FIRST HIGHWAYS OF AMERICA

by John L. Butler

Street department construction and maintenance
equipment yard, city of Burlington, Vermont.
Wilbur Collection, University of Vermont Library.

Published by

700 E. State Street • Iola, WI  54990-0001
Telephone: 715/445-2214


Library of Congress Catalog Number: 93–80094
ISBN: 0–87341–280–X
Printed in the United States of America

# Contents

# *Preface*

Automobiles, whether old or new, are useless without roads upon which to travel, and the pioneer automobiles and the roads over which they traveled have held compelling interest, bordering on passion, for me throughout most of my life. Although this story of road construction is far from complete, it is an absolutely essential part of the whole story of automotive history. Collecting information and illustrative photos about roads accompanied my restoration and subsequent driving of Model T Fords for the past thirty years and a MGTD for the past dozen.

Many individuals and agencies have helped this project come to fruition. Not the least of these are the antique automobile clubs, both local and national, through which I have been able to express my interest in old cars. The Antique Automobile Club of America published my two-part article, "Molasses to Macadam," in *Antique Automobile*, and then recognized it with their M.J. Duryea Cup Award for best historical writing for 1991. The article begins treatment of many of the subjects of this book. The *Bulb Horn*, magazine of the Veteran Motor Car Club of America, published my series of four articles, "Finding Your Way," in 1990 and 1991 issues, and then the club recognized the series with their 1991 award for Academic Research. Chapters nine and ten of *First Highways of America* are based upon this series. The *Vintage Ford*, journal of the Model T Ford Club of America, published "Model Ts in Construction," upon which chapter seven is based.

Photographs in this book come from a wide variety of sources. Of particular assistance have been the National Automotive History Collection of the Detroit Public Library and curators, the late Jim Bradley and Ron Grantz; the Western History Collection of the Denver Public Library; and The Ford Archives, especially then-archivist David R. Crippen. Similarly, the Ohio Historical Society was generous in allowing access to an amazing collection of photos made during the early years by the Ohio State Highway Department. Bill White was instrumental in my obtaining information about the Columbia River Highway and allowed use of several of his photos. I am grateful as well to many other

and allowed use of several of his photos. I am grateful as well to many other ~~and allowed use of several of his photos. I am grateful as well to many other~~ *duplicated line*
groups and individuals who have allowed me to use images from their collections.

The staff of the Media Center and Woodward Library, Austin Peay State University, assisted in many ways. Francis B. Francois, Executive Director of the American Association of State Highway and Transportation Officials, and William D. Toohey Jr., Vice President for Communications of the American Road and Transportation Builders Association, kindly read the manuscript and offered suggestions. My list of acknowledgments could not be complete without mentioning two people who got me started: Arve Peterson, in the purchase of my first Model T; and Rey Wik, author of Henry Ford and Grassroots America, who encouraged my interest in automobile and road history.

Antique car buffs come in many varieties. I am fortunate to be married to one, one who not only tolerates my hobby interests but shares them. Indeed, LuAnnette is a dedicated driver of vintage sports cars. I gratefully and lovingly dedicate this volume to her.

> "I think people are going to buy quite a passel of these little gasoline buggies and they need gasoline to make 'em go. It may be the thing of the future."
>
> -- Frank Phillips, founder of Phillips Oil Company

# Introduction

The history of the automobile has been chronicled in great detail. But the highway, the absolutely essential partner of the automobile, largely has been overlooked.

This is unfortunate. It also is somewhat surprising because, even as Americans have had a 90-year love affair with their automobiles, they likewise have had an affinity for road machinery. The yellow-colored graders, earth-movers, bulldozers, rollers, and super-sized trucks are always admired as they cut through hillsides and fill in ravines. Many of us have watched with envy as operators push aside tons of earth or rock with a bulldozer. People like road making equipment today and always have, even when the locomotive force was a pair of mules.

Americans have been the most "prone to wander" nation in history. The wedding of a quality system of highways to the technological and manufacturing skill which brought automobiles into the price range of most people, enabled that wandering to occur. The automobile became the mechanism for uninhibited, personalized and rapid movement of an independent, exploratory people. But the automobile had to have appropriate roads which would allow it to function. The early history of American roads and highways falls rather naturally into separate periods. The Connecticut Highway Commission staff in 1935 described it this way:

> Highway building, since the formation of the state highway department, naturally divides itself into three distinct epochs: from 1895 to 1913, the promotion of the good roads movement; from 1913 to 1923, an attempt to meet the demand of the public for the maximum amount of road mileage possible...; from 1923 to the present, the construction of a type road which will take care of the ever-increasing traffic....

The Connecticut pattern applied in general to eastern states. For midwestern and western states, the pattern was delayed somewhat. And certainly there are other ways of dividing highway history that can be equally meaningful.

Recognition of major events may prove even more helpful than distinguishing time periods. These surely are among the most important milestones of highway history if not the eight most important:

> Beginning manufacture of safety bicycles in the United States in 1878.
>
> Establishment of the first state highway department by the state of Maryland in 1891.
>
> Formation of the United States Office of Road Inquiry (sometimes recorded as Inquiries) as a part of the Department of Agriculture in 1893.
>
> Manufacture of that automobile model which was destined to bring autos to the mass of American people, the Model T Ford, initiated in 1908.
>
> First use of cement concrete to construct a quality, all-weather highway in Wayne County, Michigan in 1908.
>
> Movement for a coast to coast national highway, actually beginning in 1901, with successful establishment of the Lincoln Highway in 1914.
>
> Passage of the Federal Aid Highway Act by Congress in 1916.
>
> Adoption of the uniform federal highway numbering system in 1925.

With the establishment of a system of roads and highways that allowed rapid movement in any direction from any point in the country came the development of a new style of civilization, the automobile society. Strip cities built up along major highways. Then a variety of business evolved, the drive-in business, including restaurants, banks, theaters, dry cleaners, and a host of others. More recently the shopping mall, surrounded by acres of black-top paving, has become the symbol of the automobile civilization.

This volume takes a look at what came before the automobile civilization and the evolution of roads that allowed it to develop. The entire history of roads is not included. Rather, this is the history of construction of early roads and highways intended for automobile travel in the United States. Perhaps more accurately it is a picture story of the "how" and "why" of roads for horseless carriages and early automobiles. It alludes to the period of bicycles and their riders, the wheelmen, because of their great influence in getting ready for travel by automobile. Primarily, the period of 1890 to 1925 is covered. Certainly, this book is not complete; rather, it is a glimpse of a glorious period in American society, a period of expansion in personal travel.

More explicitly, this is the story of how Americans got their automobiles, and then their country, out of the mud and the dust.

# 1
# *Wheels Begin To Turn*

**L**ong after the automobile progressed from a jerking, chugging, experimental buggy into a relatively rapid and reliable means of transportation, there was nowhere to go in one. Use was pretty well limited to city streets by the absence of country roads and highways. For that matter, in many parts of the United States there was scarcely anything that could be called a "road" when one looked at the paired ruts that stretched between towns. Archer B. Hulbert took a humorous view in this anecdote from *The Future of Road-Making in America*:

> It is said that a man riding on a heavy southern road saw a hat in the mud; stopping to pick it up he was surprised to find a head of hair beneath it; then a voice came out of the ground; "Hold on, boss, don't take my hat; I've got a powerful fine mule down here somewhere if I can ever get him out!"

The way out of the mud, ruts, and dust was slow. America's early automobile drivers found that their desire for intercity roads suitable for cars to travel was mostly a dream, a dream realized only after a very considerable period of time. At the beginning of the 20th century, the automobile industry resembled the proverbial person who "was all dressed up with nowhere to go."

Automotive historians often cite advanced European technology as the reason why American motorcar development lagged behind that of the French and Germans. Although that doubtless is true, it may well be that European progress was motivated by the fact that they had somewhere to go in their automobiles. There were hundreds of miles of hard-surfaced intercity routes

**Denver Public Library, Western History Collection.**

**Denver Public Library, Western History Collection.**

in France and Germany. As early as 1895, a group of 40 cars raced 800 miles from Paris to Bordeaux and back to Paris, a distance which 10 years later could be traversed in the United States only over many days.

Roads passable for automobile travel simply did not exist in the United States in the 1890s and the early years of the 20th century. A highway authority of that period described the roads of the United States as "inferior to those of any civilized country." In considering the quality of American roads, pioneer auto manufacturer Albert Pope said, "The American who buys an automobile must pick between bad roads and worse." Roads nego-

**Denver Public Library, Western History Collection.**

tiable by horses and wagons simply would not do for the early automobiles.

Today we read and hear of thousands of accidents on roads so smooth that they allow drivers to go to sleep. Safety officials caution about the hypnotic effect of prolonged driving and watching the constant white and yellow lines on the highway. Tourists complain about the repetitious appearance of the countryside. Indeed, the travel along an interstate route can be monotonous and boring even while it is swift and smooth. But in the early days of the automobile, travel was anything but boring and the road was anything but smooth. Any journey outside the city limits was a difficult undertaking and

something of a gamble as well.

The years 1877 and 1878 had tremendous impact upon the development of roads. Automobile historians might well disagree with the selection of those years, recalling that the following year, 1879, was the time of filing the famous Selden patent, a very general patent for a gasoline-powered road vehicle. The Selden patent was eventually beaten by Henry Ford in 1911 in a series of celebrated and often bitter lawsuits. But it really was 1877 and '78 when a very substantial new need for roads developed.

Albert A. Pope began importing bicycles from England in 1877, and 1878 was the year he began manufacturing his own "Columbia" brand bicycles. These were the old high wheelers, more correctly called velocipedes or "ordinary bicycles," which had been around in England since 1873. Following their introduction, they became popular with a few riders. But only a few, for the high wheelers were hard to keep upright and exhausting to keep rolling.

Later, when the safety bicycle with wheels of equal size arrived on the scene, thousands of riders became hundreds of thousands and then millions. The new enthusiasts poured out of the cities, where there were reasonable surfaces for riding into the country on whatever roads existed — narrow, often

**Members of a cycling club, perhaps the League of America Wheelmen, posing beneath the then largest stone arch bridge in the world, near Washington, D.C., circa 1890. Library of Congress.**

steep, rutted, rough, sometimes a sea of mud and other times a cloud of choking dust -- practically none of which had a hard surface.

The joy of traveling freely under one's own power, wherever and whenever one pleased, brought about a surging demand for better roads from the cyclists. The excitement of riding inspired this short verse, originally in *The Wheelman*:

> Hurrah, hurrah for the merry wheel,
> With tires of rubber and spokes of steel;
> We seem to fly on the airy steeds
> With eagle's flight in silence speed.

The League of American Wheelmen, founded in 1880, soon became the voice of the dedicated touring cyclists. The organization's purpose was "to ascertain, defend and protect the rights of wheelmen, to encourage and facilitate tour-

Effects of truck traffic. From Anderson's *Modern Road Building and Maintenance* published by the Hercules Powder Company.

**Society folks visit Ormond Beach by bicycle and auto, circa 1910. Florida Department of Commerce, Division of Tourism.**

ing." A letter from the League to Massachusetts Congressman N. P. Banks suggested that "...your interest in public affairs will impel you to welcome any movement for the common good...the movement for better roads is becoming vigorous and prominent." Initial efforts of the wheelmen were largely ignored, partly because it tended to be a group of the "idle rich," a cycle costing $150 to $200 in those days, when the average city house cost only five to ten times that amount, and because it was a localized, New England organization. Wheelmen later channeled their efforts into education and encouragement of other groups to lobby for road improvement.

By the 1890s, public opinion, which had been indifferent to quality of roads, gradually changed. A National League for Good Roads appeared in 1892, a

Good Roads Convention occurred in Washington, D.C. in 1893, and more and more cycles were produced and sold. Four million cyclists rode those roads that existed in 1896. Hiram Percy Maxim, one of the early giants of the automobile industry, described the great contribution by the cyclists to transportation development: "The bicycle first directed men's minds to the possibility of independent, long-distance travel over the ordinary highway -- a mechanically propelled vehicle was wanted instead of a foot propelled one and we now know that the automobile was the answer."

It is interesting to note that cyclists experienced a set of problems, in addition to bad roads, which was a portent of things to come. Bicyclists were regarded with suspicion and as a menace to public safety. They were accused of "scorching," the then-current term for speeding, a thought which seems absurd to us today. But then, 20 miles per hour on a bicycle appeared fast to those on foot or even to those driving gently to church or on a shopping trip in a buggy. In some areas a bicycle rider who met a horse was required to dismount and allow the horse and rider to pass safely before continuing his cycle trip.

Later the restrictions imposed upon automobiles were even more severe. The first motor vehicle legislation in New York state required the operator of an automobile, on signal from the driver of a horse-drawn vehicle, to pull to the side of the road and wait for it to pass. If the horse was restive, the motorist had to shut off his engine. Naturally, that meant the motorist then had to get out and crank to start the machine again. The city of Mitchell, South Dakota even went so far as to pass an ordinance prohibiting automobiles within the city limits.

**Young wheelmen prepare for a ride. Clarksville/Montgomery County Museum.**

The first substantial answer to the Wheelmen's demands to remedy the deplorable road conditions came with the passage of state aid legislation in 1891 in New Jersey. "Their persistent demand and numerous publications...have done much to bring about the movement of 'good roads,' a movement that they are sustaining by all means at their command." As a result of the legislation, Middlesex County, New Jersey, constructed 10-1/2 miles of macadam highway at three separate locations in 1892. Of broader significance was action by Congress, which created the U.S. Office of Road Inquiry, a part of the Department of Agriculture, in 1893. The Office of Road Inquiry was responsible for gathering facts about the deplorable condition of U.S. roads. General Roy Stone, head of the office, estimated the cost to transport goods over then-existing roads was three times higher than it should be on good roads, caused by extra wear and tear on wagons and the draft animals which pulled them.

The office completed a road census in 1904, showing 2,151,570 miles of roads in the United States. Of this, about seven percent, roughly (in more ways than one!) 150,000 miles, could be classified as "improved," which generally meant graded and surfaced with gravel, small stones, shell, or even planks. Demonstrating vividly the difficulty of traveling those roads, improved or not, was a 1,258-mile motor tour, also conducted in 1904. The tour began on July 25 in New York City and was completed seventeen days later in St. Louis at the Louisiana Purchase Exposition. Beginning the trip were seventy-nine automobiles, and some fifty-nine managed to reach St. Louis.

A powerful new voice joined the movement for road improvement during the 1890s: the railroads. Railroad officials were convinced that better roads could extend their service areas. There were many remote regions where it was not profitable to build branch lines, but from which and to which goods needed to move. They saw good roads and wagon traffic as a means to increase their business substantially.

The beginning of free mail delivery in 1896 created another reason for good roads and provided evidence for possible benefits of highway transportation. The Rural Free Delivery system spread rapidly around the country and by 1900 was nationwide. The rural mail carrier, of course, argued for good roads, at least passable ones, and the rural people certainly appreciated receiving their mail at home. "The prospect of a daily visit from the mail man was a powerful lever to prize (pry) conservative agriculturists loose from their change-resisting attitudes."

As the age of the automobile entered the 20th century, it was the nation's farmers who exerted much of the force that moved the good roads movement into the political arena. Although some rural people were anti-automobile, and perhaps most farmers felt that way before the turn of the century, practicality won the rural population over to a new way of thinking. Farmers simply needed a faster, more efficient way to get to town for supplies and to get their products to market.

Further, farmers wanted a taste of the "good life" that they knew existed in the exciting cities. The *Journal of the Proceedings of the National Grange* in 1906 lamented, "Bad roads spell ISOLATION for the American farmer in giant letters which reach across the continent from ocean to ocean." Slow, nearly impossible transportation enforced a particular kind of limited social life upon rural Americans. Smith Haworth related in his fascinating little book, *Born Barefoot*, that:

**Ohio Historical Society's Department of Highways Collection.**

Butchering when the crisp fall days came was a gala event.... There was the roaring fire where large flat stones were heated...the 'dousing' of the butchered hog.... And best of all a supper of tenderloin. Another recreational opportunity may seem somewhat strange...the custom carried on by the younger set of 'sitting' with the dead. From stories I heard the sombre atmosphere was easily absorbed and these all night ventures in fellowship were eagerly grasped as social opportunities.

Social life in rural America had to have some relationship to work. An extremely important event was required, such as death or marriage, before one's work schedule was interrupted.

Also of tremendous importance in the good roads movement were the Glidden Tours, held from 1905 through 1913, involving hundreds of automobiles, their drivers and passengers. The Glidden Tours were competitive but were not races. Rather, they were events intended to demonstrate reliability and provide a touring opportunity for wealthy automobilists. What they proved more than anything else was the need for adequate roads before the automobile could anywhere near meet the potential it had for rapid and comfortable personal transportation.

Millionaire C.J. Glidden provided an elaborate silver trophy for the winner of the tours that bore his name, and which began with a route of some 870 miles in 1905. Starting that first year in New York City, the intrepid tourists battled their way to Bretton Woods, New Hampshire, and back. "Battled" was an appropriate term because the automobile had not yet become popular with many rural New Englanders, and they added certain pitfalls to the naturally occurring difficulties of weak tires and disastrous roads. A particularly obnoxious farmer buried a crosscut saw in the road, one of the big-toothed, two-man variety for cutting trees, and it was "discovered" by the tires of four par-

**Major Vermont road, circa 1905. Vermont Historical Society. ATX-673.**

**Leading horses and buggies by a motor car, circa 1906. National Automotive History Collection, Detroit Public Library.**

**Getting some help in 1907. National Automotive History Collection, Detroit Public Library.**

ticipating cars. The press took note of the tour when the *Manchester* (New Hampshire) *Union* described the touring group as an "unmitigated nuisance." Also of note during these liberated and liberating times is the fact that one of the drivers among the 34 participating cars was a woman. She hadn't gone far before driving her White steamer off a ten-foot bridge while attempting to avoid a problem which her male counterparts created. They heaved her car back on the road, and she completed the run.

Subsequent Glidden Tours went in other directions, explored roads even worse than those encountered on the initial tour, and did much to convince the general public that intercity travel could be accomplished by automobile. Just as important, the tours helped convince the public that it was worthwhile to spend tax money to build better roads.

Tours conducted on a more localized basis similarly were designed to illustrate the utility of the automobile and were designated as Reliability Runs or

**Most roads included an abundance of puncture material. Tennessee State Archives.**

**The lifetime of a tire in 1909 seldom exceeded 2,000 miles. National Automotive History Collection, Detroit Public Library.**

28

29

Endurance Runs. The Sept. 26, 1912, issue of *Motor Age* listed no less than four such events, including one thus described:

> The sensational reliability run of the Chicago Motor Club which proposes to encircle Lake Michigan...is attracting the attention of the western motoring public because of the boldness of the enterprise and the difficulties that are being encountered by the pathfinding [party]...it is almost wild country, the road winding through picturesque woods. The going is none too good but still negotiable, while the country penetrated abounds in wild animals...they heard bears and wolves in the underbrush and it was necessary to fire their guns to scare away the animals."

Some tours were designed just to provide entertainment and were called sociability runs. "The first sociability tour of any proportions to be run out of Cincinnati took place Saturday...175 cars and more than 800 people took

Automobile club outing, circa 1910. Colorado Historical Society.

part...The route lay from Cincinnati to the Dayton Automobile Club and return...prizes were awarded to those drivers making the best average time."

Automobile clubs sprang up across the nation during the first ten years of the century and played a prominent role, as did the cyclist's clubs before them, in mobilizing public opinion in favor of road development. Local auto clubs in a number of eastern cities joined together to form the American Automobile Association in 1902, providing a broader-based voice for the automobilists. Most of the clubs in the Midwest, unlike their eastern big-city predecessors, where touring opportunities and social activities were featured, were organized for practical reasons as illustrated in a newspaper report in 1908: "The principle object of the organization is to make a systematic effort to improve the roads in Grant County and in this part of the state, and to cooperate with other like organizations to secure much needed good roads legislation at the coming session of the legislature." Another club in the Midwest, also in

**National Automotive History Collection, Detroit Public Library.**

**Early suspension bridge in Nashville. Note $5 fine for driving faster than a walk. Tennessee State Archives.**

1908, claimed an additional purpose, "that those who drive autos and who violate the speed and road laws should be promptly and vigorously punished." The newspaper article which reported this included a bit of editorializing about the good roads movement: "The improvement of the roads in the county is not alone a matter of interest to those who own a chug-wagon. Every farmer who drives to market, and every townsman who drives into the country, as well as every retail merchant, is interested."

Many of the local automobile clubs were organized before states even became involved in highway construction. Although New Jersey allocated the first state monies for highway construction in 1891, and Massachusetts established the first state highway department in 1893, the majority of state highway departments were established by state legislatures between 1905 and 1917.

Of significant note in a day in which the populace expects its government to perform many functions for it, these automobile clubs were apparently willing to put their money where their mouths were. One of the midwestern clubs mentioned earlier split costs of road building with townships. The Minneapolis

**Road crew with teams and scrapers. Tennessee State Archives.**

Automobile Club purchased and manned equipment such as horse-drawn sprinkling wagons and graders. The Louisville Automobile Club repaired some of the worst mud holes in their area and then erected signs that said, "This hole filled by the Louisville Automobile Club."

The work of the clubs did not prove to be enough to provide passable roads for the club members. Their automobiles were capable of long distance travel, but the fact was that highway development lagged behind automobile development. Motor Age in 1899 opined that "the motor vehicle industry would starve if it should wait for road improvement." That journal also warned manufacturers and owner/drivers: "Don't preach that motor vehicles depend on roads. They don't. They depend on good suitable construction to negotiate any kind of road surface and on perfectly reliable motors." But such a statement just wasn't true. No automobile of that time, or any time, was so constructed that it could handle mountains, canyons, fine sand, or boggy areas. And purchas-

Mt. Pisgah Auto Road Near Asheville, N.C.

**Mt. Pisgah auto road near Asheville, North Carolina, in 1913. Library of Congress.**

ers then and later wanted to enjoy travel in their cars rather than fight with impossible roads. John B. Rae, in his *The American Automobile*, saw a synergistic effect of auto upon road and road upon auto:

> Highway development had the unforeseeable effect of touching off a race between road and vehicle that is still in progress, with the vehicle consistently ahead. Not only was the number of cars on the highways steadily increasing, but as the roads got better, owners of motor vehicles were encouraged to use them more freely. Old roads were rebuilt and new ones were added; the result seemed to be merely that traffic got progressively heavier. In addition, better roads encouraged automotive engineers to design faster cars and heavier trucks so that a new highway was likely obsolescent by the time it was finished.

**Breaking sod to replace two ruts across the prairie with a real road. South Dakota State Historical Society.**

Automobile drivers soon were well aware that "the average automobile is better than the average road," even though their average cars in the early years may have had only one or two cylinders and rode on tires without any tread. Whatever year one might choose to observe, quality of automobile technology exceeded quality of highway technology.

At first sight it seems incredible that in a country so progressive as ours the condition of the common roads should be over a half century behind that of the old world!
-- *Scientific American*, June 30, 1900

"If it wasn't for automobiles," she says, "I wouldn't have to pay any more taxes than I used to. But they must have carpet roads to run on and I have got to pay for the roads."
-- *Ford Times*, 1913

Macaulay says that of all inventions, the alphabet and printing press alone excepted, those inventions which abridge distance have done most for the civilization of our species. A nation, or an age of civilization, is perhaps more easily judged and understood by the character and extensiveness of its roads, than by any other symbol of progress.
-- Colonel Albert A. Pope, Oct. 17, 1889

## Average Motorist's Signal Code
## is a Dangerous One

Have you ever stopped to consider the signal code of the average motor car driver? It is a very simple code and not in any sense difficult to acquire. It follows:

To indicate a right turn -- stick out your hand.

To indicate a left turn -- stick out your hand.

To indicate that you are about to stop -- stick out your hand.

To indicate that you are about to back -- stick out your hand.

To emphasize your conversation with your fellow passenger -- stick out your hand.

To flick the ashes off your cigar -- stick out your hand.

This is a generally accepted code. Under the circumstances it is remarkable that accidents are not more frequent, although the present toll in human life and limb is appalling and steadily growing. -- Fred Caley

# 2
# *Starting to Build*

**J**ust how significant the automobile, truck, and, of course, the highway, would become was still unclear except in the minds of a few visionaries. In his novel, *Excuse My Dust*, Bellamy Partridge includes this conversation, which is prophetic...but inaccurate:

> Roscoe, you've had a chance to study the motor vehicle at first hand. What's your opinion of it? Do you think it will ever reach the point where it will supplant the horse?
>
> "Never," said Roscoe emphatically. "It will never supplant the horse any more than the bicycle has supplanted the horse. And I'll tell you why -- the motor car is adapted to sport, not utility, and it never can be adapted to utility....
>
> In the first place, it's not reliable enough," said Roscoe. "Of course they may be able to fix the mechanical part of it in time; but the moment the motor car rolls off the city pavement, it's a fish out of water. And it's hardly likely that just to make the going easy for a rich man's toy the roads of this country are going to be turned into pavements. Think what that would cost."
>
> Andy shook his head. "It would bankrupt the nation."

But in spite of the frightful roads or, throughout much of the nation, the absence of roads, some audacious automobilists set out to see the country.

The early, relatively simple automobiles, although not yet marvels of mechanical knowledge, were tough. They had to be to survive the rigors of cross-country travel. As early as 1903, three automobiles were driven all the

Rock and puncheon road, Pine Mountain, Letcher County, Kentucky. Kentucky Historical Society.

**To California and Return, picture believed to be taken in 1905. Denver Public Library, Western History Collection.**

way across the United States, a two-cylinder Winton, single-cylinder Packard and single-cylinder Oldsmobile. However, it took 63 days for the Winton, which was the first, and many of the nearly 6,000 miles (it required almost double today's mileage in order to locate a passable route) were not on a road at all.

But the roads, or perhaps we should call them routes, were even tougher than the cars. The difficulties encountered in driving across western South Dakota in a 1905 single-cylinder Cadillac were recorded by Peter Norbeck, later a governor and U.S. Senator:

> There is no question that I drove the first automobile from the Missouri (river) to the Black Hills. I drove in the spring in a single-cylinder Cadillac... The old machine required frequent

On the main highway, Denver to Albuquerque, in 1913. Denver Public Library, Western History Collection.

43

repairs and adjustments. We left Fort Pierre at daylight and got out 88 miles that evening, having had more or less mud to contend with during most of the afternoon. A real spring rain came on and we remained at a ranch house for a couple of days."

**A broken axle and other problems. National Automotive History Collection, Detroit Public Library.**

The next thirty miles for Norbeck were through gumbo aided by a team of horses; it required both horse and horseless power to go those thirty miles. Crossing the Cheyenne River during spring flood was a task with considerable risk. Three riders on horseback assisted, pulling the Cadillac through the water at a gallop. Norbeck recalled, "The machine pounded onto the rocks in the riverbed. It was fortunate indeed that the machine was not smashed...."

As road builders initiated construction at many locations throughout the country, they employed a variety of techniques and materials. The advent of the automobile, of course, raised the standards necessary for road construction. L.W. Page of the U.S. Office of Public Roads stated, "We have lived so long with our earth roads at their worst that we fail to see that vast improvement is possible. This, too, need not jeopardize further improvements and still better

Toll gate for "Million Dollar Highway," Ouray, Colorado. Coe Library, University of Wyoming.

45

roads, such as gravel or macadam. A good earth road is the stepping stone to a hard road."

Pioneer motorists who felt (literally) the need for those hard roads were inspired to concoct such literary gems as:

The Roads are impassable
Hardly Jackassable;
I think those that travel 'em
Should turn out and gravel 'em."

And indeed, some of them did turn out to "gravel 'em," such as the Minneapolis Automobile Club mentioned earlier. In Wyoming, "members of 'Good Roads Clubs' in many towns devoted free time to volunteer work on the roads, removing rocks, filling ruts, and repairing bridges. They regularly carried sacks of gravel on their running boards, prepared to stop and dump the gravel into the first mudhole."

**Kentucky Historical Society.**

Volunteer efforts were important in North Carolina in 1913 when two days were designated as holidays from normal work and everyone was asked "to shoulder his shovel and march out and strike a blow for progress." Similar "Good Roads Days" had been attempted elsewhere, but just how valuable such events were at actually improving the roads, utilizing total amateurs as they did, is subject to some question. One critic observed, "It seems to me that it is a backward step in good roads building to have everybody -- inexperienced and otherwise -- fooling with the roads."

Some road experts found such practice to be overly like the nearly universal practice in this country during the 1800s, and up through 1910 in some regions, of "working out" the road tax. During that

**Photo by U.S. Forest Service.**

period, roads were the responsibility of the township, and each man was expected to pay a road tax in the form of labor upon the roads adjacent to his farmland. Usually from two to four days per year were required, but most of the work was performed half-heartedly and with little or no knowledge about how to build or improve a road. "Working out the tax" did not provide an adequate work force for road construction. About this practice Oklahoma's first Highway Commissioner said:

> Did you ever hear of a man putting in an honest day's work on the roads? The idea of a man working out his road tax is the poorest piece of foolishness ever sanctioned by law. He might as well work out his school tax. Tell him, 'This is your day to teach -- go down to school now and work out your school tax teaching the children.' What does he know about teaching? Nothing, of course! But he knows as much about teaching as about road-building. Every man ought to be required to pay his road tax in cash, like other taxes. Then the law should provide for the employment of a competent engineer and experienced road-builders who know how to construct roads along practical lines."

Muscle power for building roads, both men and animals. Photo by U.S. Forest Service.

**Preparing to grade a Vermont highway. Vermont Historical Society ATX-218.**

Similarly, the U.S. Department of Public Roads said:

> The road work of this country is inefficient and inadequate. Pennsylvania, for example, had 3,000 townships, and the supervisor of each township was the road boss of that unit. There are probably 100,000 of these township road officers in the United States, each one exercising separate authority with no ranking head to direct groups of them. What would a railroad do if each of its section bosses were permitted to buy all the material for constructing and maintaining his little piece of road?

However, "Good Roads Days" during August 1913, as set aside by Missouri's Governor Elliott Major, brought out 300,000 men and accomplished work equivalent to $1 million if it had been done by contract. The Missouri Highway Commissioner admitted, "As to actual results of improvement it was not thought very much would be accomplished, but the willingness with which the

**Six mule team and grader. Tennessee State Archives.**

people responded far exceeded what had been expected." A significant by-product, which had not been anticipated, was the new interest level of farmers and other citizens in their roads, roads in which they then had a sweat invest-ment. Those citizens subsequently placed pressure on their legislators for funding of road construction. Perhaps the greatest benefit of good roads days was in education and in attitude adjustment.

*Good Roads*, a weekly journal of road and street contracting, editorialized:

> The work done in Missouri on the 'good roads days' appears to have been not the unorganized, haphazard work which might have been done had each man who worked on the days when the farmers of New York, New England and other states in the East worked out their road taxes. On the contrary, a large part of it appears to have been performed by thoroughly organized forces under competent supervision, working not only willingly but with enthusiasm."

51

52

Without doubt, when effectively organized and where the road types were earth, gravel or even macadam, the volunteer labor was able to accomplish a great deal. In the more sparsely populated regions of the country where there wasn't much of a tax base upon which to depend for large road contracts, many miles of road were made passable for automobiles during such work days. Included were some projects of startling magnitude.

The greatest piece of road building the world ever witnessed was pulled off in Iowa last week when, in the short space of one single hour, a line of road 380 miles in length and stretching entirely across the state of Iowa was put in the most perfect condition of any road west of the Mississippi River.

Cover of *The Highway Magazine* for August 1920 salutes a "Good Road Day" in North Carolina.

Obviously such an accomplishment required months of preparation. The Iowa political structure was employed to recruit the 10,000 farmers who used their own teams, plows, scrapers and drags to shape up a "river to river" road that extended from Davenport west to Council Bluffs. It was a bipartisan job with both Democratic and Republican county committees urging their men to be on the job.

A similar feat in Kansas was inspired in part by the Iowans but was organized primarily by one man, H.G. James, an Independence newspaper publisher. The twenty-mile stretch of road between Independence and Coffeyville was rebuilt in a single day by the citizens of those cities and the farmers who lived between. One mile of road was built ahead of time at each end of the route in order to prove to everyone the seriousness of the project. Then

**From time to time, there were challenges. Kansas State Historical Society.**

on Nov. 15, 1910, volunteer road builders rebuilt the road. It was no easy task for the unseasoned constructors.

> "I take great pride in saying that Judge Flannelly and his lawyer and court house assistants wore blisters on their hands, but they worked steadily until night, blasting and digging the rock out, making two side gutters in solid stone, cracking rock in the middle of the road and covering it with clay, and filling in the depression at the foot of the hill until as by magic, an eyesore for half a century was transformed into a fine roadway…"

All along the way between these hills were scores of teams and men plowing, scraping, dragging. A great steam traction engine puffed and snorted and tore up the ground and dragged it to the center of the road.

It was a great sight. Try to imagine, if you can, men and teams with road building machinery of every description lining the highway for eighteen miles between these two cities.

Here were lawyers and doctors, preachers and politicians, day laborers and millionaires, bankers and clerks, printers and

55

Favorite photo background was (and often is) the family car. Mr. and Mrs. Fox Turner. Fayette County, Kentucky.

Heavy traffic in Asheville, North Carolina. Pack Memorial Public Library, Asheville, North Carolina.

mechanics, friends and enemies, shoulder to shoulder, without wage or price, working in a great public enterprise for the common weal. It was inspiring.

During the summer of 1915, all Kansans were urged to join in road work on Good Roads Days for Kansas. Colorado celebrated a Good Roads Day with hard labor on the roads by her citizens on May 14, 1915. The Denver Times for that day published a picture of then-Governor Carlson at work with the sub-headline, "Governor Carlson sets example for whole state by substituting pick and shovel for dignity."

Continuing on through the early '20s, "graveling bees" and other volunteer road building efforts were commonplace in those states where highway construction under state auspices had not yet improved the majority of highways. The labor of citizens who wanted a better way to travel played a genuine, although small, role in American road development.

Collapse of steel bridge, June, 1918, under heavy load, Marion County, Ohio. Ohio Historical Society.

The first "automobile" in Thermopolis, Wyoming. Note hard rubber tires on this commercial vehicle. Wyoming State Archives, Museums and Historical Department.

# 3
# *Roads and Rhetoric*

**D**evelopment of good roads was not entirely a process accomplished in the country where construction was going on. Much of that development had to occur in legislative chambers, in newspaper editorials, in endless meetings, conventions, general agitation and molding of public opinion. Indeed, the building of roads was very much a political process. Too much so for Carl Fisher, builder of the Indianapolis Speedway, who wrote to publisher Elbert Hubbard: "As you know, Mr. Hubbard, the highways of America are built chiefly of politics, whereas the proper material is crushed rock or concrete." In another letter to Hubbard, Fisher said, "Of agitating good roads there is no end, and perhaps this is as it should be, but I think you'll agree that it is high time to agitate less and build more."

But the agitation would prevail for many years, and it apparently was a necessary process; rhetoric dominated over construction for a long time. Massachusetts Senator Charles Sumner's statement made several decades earlier was quoted again and again by orators promoting road improvement: "The road and the schoolmaster are the two most important agents in advancing civilization." President William McKinley, in a message to Congress, added his comment: "There is a wide-spread interest in the improvement of our public highways at the present time, and the Department of Agriculture is co-operating with the people in each locality in making the best possible roads." In his inaugural address in 1902, a midwestern governor summarized the arguments other orators expounded in hundreds of separate speeches:

> People generally are beginning to realize that good roads not
> only have a positive money value to the farmers and to the

Kentucky Historical Society.

townspeople, but a social and moral value by virtue of the convenience, comfort and refining influences which good roads diffuse throughout the rural regions. Good roads, like good streets, make habitations along them desirable. Good roads economize time and force in transportation of products. Good roads reduce the wear and tear on horses and wagons. A farm twenty miles from town, on a good road, is for all practical purposes no farther from market than another farm ten miles distant on a poor road. Good roads raise the value of farm lands and the products of the farm. It has been carefully estimated that 99 percent of the tonnage handled by railroad, steamboat or express must be carried in a wagon over a highway. It is evident that the problem of good roads, while of primary importance to the farmer, is one of tremendous importance to the general public.

**Poudre River Road, Laramie County, Colorado, was built with convict labor. National Automotive History Collection, Detroit Public Library.**

**Amateur road workers -- "when we worked out our road tax." Tennessee State Archives.**

The same governor attacked the practice of working out one's road tax:

> I would recommend the abolition of the primeval custom of "working out" the poll and road tax. This custom originated at a time when money was scarce and the scattered pioneers were desperately in need of some kind of trail through the wilderness.

Good roads conventions and rallies sprang up everywhere. There were national meetings and local meetings, state meetings and county meetings. The theme was always the same: Get us some roads whereon we can travel with reasonable speed and safety. A typical convention reported its main objective as "the endorsement and promotion of a cross-state highway of standard design" and, as was true for most such proposed roads, they wanted it to be a link in a highway which crossed other states. As usual, "many able addresses were made, all endorsing the 'Good Roads' movement, which has now received tangible recognition by most of the states of the union..." One individual good roads advocate from the same state was so dedicated to his persuasive passion that he started a newspaper to "spread the gospel of good roads."

At the Second Annual [national] Good Roads Convention in 1909, it was clear that there were two dominant groups involved in the deliberations there. One was the American Automobile Association representing mostly city dwellers who had no interest in country roads until acquiring an automobile and then desiring someplace to go in that car. The other was the National Grange representing farmers who, by this time, were acquiring cars in great numbers. Prior to this time, the country dwellers, overwhelmed by work through most of the year, generally accepted the fact that they were isolated. Until there was a means of overcoming isolation, namely the automobile, there wasn't much reason to get excited about improving the roads. It took too long to go anywhere by horse and buggy. There were some other organizations present at that national roads convention and at other similar gatherings. The American

**Muscle power, both man and animal. Tennessee State Archives.**

Enthusiastic workers. Ohio Historical Society's Department of Highways Collection.

Curved dash Oldsmobile at Nashville Fairgrounds. Tennessee State Archives.

Road Builders Association, a group of contractors, the National Association of Automobile Manufacturers, and the American Motor Car Manufacturers' Association had obvious interests in what was going on and lent enthusiastic support.

But the spirit wasn't always unity and harmony. Controversies arose over types of road to be constructed, who should pay for the roads, and where principal routes should be laid out. During a major meeting for determination of the route through Kansas of the New York to San Francisco "Santa Fe Trail," opposing factions rallied with orators, signs and even bands. A musical battle ensued.

> When a speaker of one delegation attempted to speak, the opposition bands opened up with a roar. The bedlam of noises was increased when some of the delegates sent out for tin pans, upon which they beat with sticks; others had kazoos.

Still the movement gathered momentum. By December 1912, Ben W. Wood, secretary of the South Dakota Good Roads Association, asked the question that was in the minds of many. Had the highway movement, even though it had brought about great progress, run its course? "Is the present good road contention and agitation a fad? -- or political sugar used by the professional to sweeten the minds of and, to an extent, control the actions of the voter?" Wood wondered if it would follow the fashion of all fads and become out of date and soon fade away.

In many speeches and letters to editors of South Dakota newspapers, Wood made the case for better roads an economic case. "Building good roads is virtually the tilling of the soil for the production of a certain crop -- a crop which is reputed to be the greatest crop harvested in the United States today -- the tourist crop." Wood noted that tourists were taking their automobiles to the West and were leaving millions of dollars behind, some $11 million in Colorado the previous year (1911). "If we can give them a traversable highway," he believed the automobilists would spend some of their time, and money, in the Black Hills and Badlands of his state.

Although the rhetoric was essential, the single major force for progress in road construction was the placement of responsibility for roads at higher governmental levels. Not much planning for the future occurred when responsibility lay with the township where there was little vision of what the future held for transportation by automobile and truck. Turning responsibility over to counties was a giant step forward, but it resulted in checkerboard development. Some counties made tremendous progress, while in other counties the

"road tax" system continued. This resulted in excellent macadam roads merging into a pair of muddy paths when one crossed a county line.

State and federal involvements were two further steps in the progression of highway responsibility, each of which brought about extensive improvement in planning and coordination of construction. With planning and coordination came state and federal highway systems, a network of continuous, interconnecting routes, allowing for safe and comfortable auto transportation over long distances.

As is true for so many aspects of American life, progress in the matter of highways was impossible except as a political process. An Oklahoma legislator commented about the significance of state planning and a state system of highways: "If the present legislature should do no more than give Oklahoma a good system of road laws it could return home knowing that it had rendered

the greatest possible service to the state." At the national level, bills were introduced in Congress year after year by visionaries without getting a great deal of support. An article in 1913 in *Ford Times* lamented, "That the government should take a leading part in road building seems to be almost so obvious that it scarcely need be mentioned, and yet, obvious as it is, the federal government has been laggardly in recognizing this fact." *Ford Times* was a free magazine published by the Ford Motor Company and, for many years, did not produce an issue without a section titled "Good Roads."

Albert Pope, the highly successful early automobile manufacturer, as early as 1906 wrote to the then-governor of New Mexico, Herbert Hagerman, concerning the importance of the federal government taking a hand in highway planning:

> As States have advanced their interests by the betterment of public highways, so the entire Union may be enriched by a proper system of through roads. I doubt if anyone would question the value of this movement, and the one mooted question, therefore, seems to be the method of procedure.
>
> I would esteem it a great privilege to have from you an expression of opinion on the advisability of Federal Aid and Federal control in the building and upkeep of some of the main arteries of travel.

But as is always the case, not everyone was in agreement that there should be federal involvement in the matter of highway development. An editorial in *Popular Mechanics*, the kind of magazine which usually supported automobile and other mechanized development, in discussing the appropriation of $3 million in 1909 by the state of Pennsylvania for a good road from Philadelphia to Pittsburgh, said:

> The plan, however, is to be regretted. In the first place it is not needed. There is not now, nor is there likely to be, any considerable amount of trans-state freight traffic for such a road. All classes of freight are being moved by the railroads at rates which make hauling on highways prohibitive.

But, as we now know, that condition didn't last very long. And there were many people in the two cities who would like to drive to the other. In 1913, the *Christian Science Monitor* editorialized in a similar vein in reference to federal participation:

**Oil spreader and Pathfinder car for the 1908 Glidden Tour. National Automotive History Collection, Detroit Public Library.**

> The national government does not need to seek new opportunities for spending. Its treasury is not bursting with plenty. And if the government is to mark any limit to what it undertakes, it would seem the highest prudence to leave the making of roads to the states, the cities and the towns.

As things developed, both points of view received their due. Federal funding became a reality, but those funds were distributed to the states, and it was at that level where routes were selected and systems put together.

Federal financing for highways began in a very limited way as the result of an appropriation which passed Congress in 1912. A sum of $500,000 was granted to the Secretary of Agriculture who, with the counsel of the Postmaster General, was to improve the rural roads used by postal carriers. The pro-

Gravel Pit Cave-in
Ross Co.
1926

**Ohio Historical Society's Department of Highways Collection.**

This steel bridge collapsed when struck by an automobile. Ohio Historical Society's Department of Highways Collection.

gram resulted in construction of some 425 miles of roads in seventeen states. As early as 1903, the Brownlow-Latimer Federal Good Roads Bill had been introduced in Congress. But it died in committee, and national involvement in road building was still years in coming.

Federal aid on a truly national basis came with the passage of the Federal-Aid Road Act, which became law on July 11, 1916. The act recognized that quality roads were essential to the national welfare. It was for the good of the nation that mechanized transportation, other than railroads, be available. Therefore, provision of good highways was believed to be a national responsibility as well as a local one.

A rather substantial sum for the times, $75 million, was to be spent by the states over five years. Each state had to match its allocation on a 50:50 basis, and the money had to be spent only on a group of "primary" highways which could constitute no more than seven percent of that state's highways. Apportionment of monies to the states was based upon population, area and miles of rural postal delivery routes. One of the important provisions of the act was the requirement that every participating state have a highway department. But in 1916, there were still seventeen states having no state agency for highway construction. When the year 1918 began, all states had met this condition, thereby guaranteeing the complete transition from township to county to state control of highway construction.

Road building under state auspices and supported by federal aid moved much more rapidly than before and reached a comparative fervor during the 1920s. The $75 million allocated for the first five years of the Federal-Aid Road Act was matched by a like amount for the single year 1922.

Equally as severe a problem for the early builders of automobile roads in the United States was the problem of distance. In a country where single states of the then forty-five (Oklahoma achieved statehood in 1907 and Arizona and New Mexico in 1912) were as large as entire European nations, but often with only 1/50th or 1/100th of the population, it was a massive task to connect our relatively more distant cities with hard-surfaced roads. And, of course, with distance came the problem of cost. How could they pay for the cost of quality roads, especially such long roads? And how could they do it rapidly? The better roads that existed in European countries had been built over many decades. In contrast to the astronomical expense of constructing a mile of divided, controlled-access highway today, grading a narrow earth road then was cheap. However, when one considers the organization available to plan, organize and finance construction of highways today and compares it with organizational structure for highway building that existed in 1900 or 1910,

New Mexico Highway Department.

74

**Early 1920s car traveling through Oregon forest. Bill White collection.**

completion of a passable dirt road then was much more notable than completion of another section of Interstate highway now.

Following the successful development of railroad service in the 1830s, highway construction essentially was ignored for fifty years until the Wheelmen became organized. The period from 1890 to 1910 has been characterized as the "golden age" of the railroads, and, indeed, it was a grand and prosperous time for the railroads. But as the year 1900 rolled around, significant new competition was in sight. There was just the beginning of a need for roads suitable for automobile travel. But that need grew and grew.

Politics and lobbying, automobile clubs, men who delivered the mail, sporting motorists who drove elaborate Mercedes and Daimlers, and above all, common people who wanted a better life -- all these helped mushroom the cry for good roads until it was an overpowering demand. America and Americans were about to respond to that demand, but already they were a half century behind.

Resolved, That the National Grange favor a general policy of good roads construction by the various municipalities, counties and States, and,
Resolved, That we favor legislation by Congress making liberal Federal appropriations for the improvement of the public highways of the country, these appropriations to be expended in such manner as Congress may prescribe.
-- Committee of Public Highways of the National Grange, 1908

As the Mound Builders were the highest expression of prehistoric man, so the Road Builder becomes the highest and best product of modern civilization. If cleanliness is next to godliness, then good roads are a means of grace.
 -- Howard H. Gross in "Highways and Civilization," part of Modern Road Building, Transactions of the First Congress of American Road Builders

Hordes of autos now remind us
That we should build our roads to stay,
And departing leave behind us
Kind that rains don't wash away.

When our children pay the mortgage
Father's made to haul their loads,
They'll not have to ask the question,
Here is the bonds but where's the roads?
-- Custer Battlefield Highway News' parody of Longfellow's poem

# 4
# *Just Parallel Ruts*

The vast majority of roads available for auto travel during the first two decades of the 20th century were earth roads. The U.S. Office of Road Inquiry's 1904 census revealed over two million miles of "highway," but only 153,662 miles were surfaced with any hard material. That means that some ninety-three percent of the so-called highways in the United States were just plain dirt. The larger part of the remaining seven percent was surfaced with gravel; the mileage paved with asphalt, concrete, or brick was minuscule by comparison. A Connecticut Highway Department report lamented, "Although there were some paved streets in each city and in the thickly settled areas, in between, the roads were muddy in wet weather, dusty in dry weather and rough practically all of the time."

Dirt roads ranged in quality from two parallel paths with grass in the center, and no engineering, to graded roads with good drainage and an occasional smooth surface just after grading. Engaged in a transcontinental test drive in one of his cars, Henry Joy, president of the Packard Motor Car Company, asked his Omaha dealer for directions to the road west. "There isn't any," was the answer. "Then how do I go?" asked Joy. "Follow me and I'll show you." They drove westward until they came to a wire fence. "Just take down the fence and drive on and when you come to the next fence, take that down and go on again." "A little farther," said Mr. Joy, "and there were no fences, nothing but two ruts across the prairie." Travelers going any significant distance spent most of their trips enduring dirt and gravel roads and were very thankful when they had gravel. Dirt roads were especially dominant in the broad spaces of the Midwest and West. By 1906, in Minnesota, there were 79,000 miles of alleged roads, 67 miles of which were hard-surfaced, 6,179 graveled,

New Mexico Highway Department.

**Horsepower of two varieties. New Mexico Highway Department.**

79

**Split-log drag. From Frost's *The Art of Roadmaking* published in 1910.**

and 73,000 plus dirt. In 1912, the state of Idaho "covered the mud" with its first graveled road. By 1918, Idaho had progressed to the point where there were five miles of paved highway within the state boundaries. In 1914, Wyoming still could not designate any miles of hard surfaced roads. Just to the south in Colorado, that state's first highway department (1909) was impressive with words if not with their pavement, stating, "good roads lighten the burdens and boost the fortunes of all mankind. All of their 5,042 miles of designated state highways in 1914 still were gravel or earth surfaced.

Much of the smoothing and maintenance of earth roads was accomplished by a rather simple tool, the King split-log drag. It was a homemade implement, consisting of a cedar, elm, maple, or walnut log, about seven or eight feet long, split lengthwise, with the two halves "stood on edge" about two-and-a-half or three feet apart, and connected to each other by iron pipe or wooden cross beams. Planks were placed across the drag's connecting beams for a driver to stand on. Pulled by a team of horses or mules, or sometimes by a single horse, the King drag had more to do with keeping roads passable for automobiles during the first two decades of this century than any other implement.

The first annual report of the Department of Public Roads of the Commonwealth of Kentucky in 1912 reported, "For maintenance the grading machine

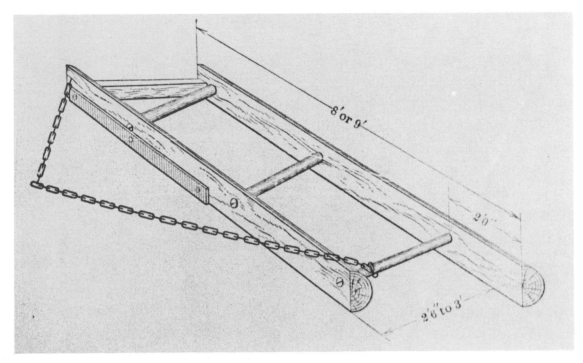

Construction diagram for a split-log drag.

Two large wooden drags in operation. Ohio Historical Society's Department of Highways Collection.

**Setting a drag made of steel plate, which could be towed at high speed by a truck.**

is of value when the condition of the road is very bad, but the Split Log Drag is the one best implement for keeping a good road good." *Modern Road Building* further complimented the drag: "With the drag properly built and its use understood, the maintenance of earth and gravel roads becomes a simple and inexpensive matter."

The way in which the drag operated was described in *The American Road*:

> "Clays and most soils will puddle and set very hard if worked when wet. The drag is essentially a puddling machine. After each rain and while the earth is still plastic, but not sticky enough to adhere to the drag, one or two trips up and down the road is made with it. Only a small amount of earth is moved, just enough to fill the ruts and depressions and smooth over the surface with a thin layer of plastic clay, which packs hard under passing traffic and leaves the road smooth and hard if of the right material. The next rain, finding no ruts and depressions in which to collect, runs off, affecting the surface but little....drag, drag, and then drag a little more if you want to insure good roads."

A tremendous amount of dragging of roads actually occurred, not only by local and county road workers, but sometimes by volunteer associations, even over some substantial distances. The Santa Fe Trail Association developed a plan for dragging the road from Kansas City to Albuquerque:

> "In brief the plan is to drag the road on both sides and in the middle for a distance of more than 1,000 miles. Never before has such a thing been attempted in the United States."

> "We will have six drags of special size built for us," he continued. "These will be attached to automobiles, three of which will take one side of the road and three the other side. In this way we will make a clean sweep."

The Waubonsic Trail Association purchased drags, which they asked their members to tow behind their cars on a highway across southern Iowa. Their clever slogan was "You Auto-drag."

**Colorado Historical Society.**

Actual construction in those early days didn't turn out to be as careful and precise as an engineering textbook would have taught the builders. Some of the earliest construction in the vast reaches of rolling plains between the Missouri River and Black Hills of South Dakota was described by Louis J. Jensen. He began as a foreman for road building in 1912 with a wage of 30 cents per hour. A bridge had been constructed over the Cheyenne River; a highway designated by its promoters as the "Black Hills and Yellowstone Trail" was to cross it. Each township along the route was to build its section of the road. Township boards selected the route, and the foreman laid it out; "there was no surveying instruments used -- it was just a matter of going where the going was easiest."

> "On October 9, 1912, I started the road from Lake Flatt down the hill toward the Cheyenne River. I started it with a spade, spading out a trail along the side of the hill where I finally made it safe for one horse, pulling a left-hand plow, could walk. The trail followed hogback or ridge all the way down to the foot of the hills. Our road equipment consisted of walking plows pulled by two horses, fresnos pulled by four horses and one road grader pulled by four horses. Later that fall we had a trail that could be used by tourists and this was the first tourist route through this area...its only markers were black and yellow rings painted on fence posts and telephone poles, and sometimes on a board tacked to a fence. A few cars drove over the trail the first fall, but the road was not finished until August of 1913."

Determination of the best course for the early roads to follow was seldom done with scientific accuracy. A road crew working in Kansas reported, "We staked out the roads by sighting from one cornerstone to another. We used our naked eye and a tall pole with a little flag on the end of it."

Lack of a dependable, hard surface on the roads of 1900 through 1910 had considerable influence on automobile design and, for that matter, on the entire economy of the automotive industry. The class of automobiles referred to as "high wheelers" was so designed as to provide with their large wheels a high clearance over obstructions in the road. Usually the major problem of clearance for early cars was the ridge of earth and mud between two deep ruts. International's Autobuggy; Holsman; Schacht; Black; and Sears, Roebuck and Company's Motorbuggy all had considerable road clearance, and even the cars with smaller wheels had much greater clearance than today's models. Stanley Edmunds recorded travel experiences in his family's 1904

Cadillac, noting that the car often became "hung up" on the center ridge of deeply rutted roads. Then forward progress stopped and the task of digging out began. By backing up and then cutting ramps into the sides of the ruts, one usually could get out of the impasse. Of course, this applied when the ruts were more or less dry or at least firm. In wet weather the only answer was a tow job, and in those days that meant the nearest farmer and "Old Dobbin." Edmunds recalled a fairly long trip in the '04 Cadillac, some 150 miles, which involved a crossing of the Missouri River by ferry. The hill descending to the ferry was long, but not too steep.

> "I happened to look back, and seeing a cloud of trailing black smoke, I knew something was wrong. When we stopped and went to investigate, we found both brakes were afire and blazing nicely. For brakes the Cadillac had a brake drum bolted to the rear wheel spokes and the brake shoe was a piece of rubber belting...after cooling the brakes we crossed the river on the ferry but our troubles were not over. The road was very close to the river and badly rutted. In attempting to straddle the ruts, father drove too close to the river, the right wheels caved off a piece of the bank which in turn caused the car to swing crosswise with the front wheels hanging over the water. Luckily the rear axle dragged and caught on the center ridge and saved us from serious accident."

It was unusual for the rut and ridge condition of roads to prove beneficial as was true in this case. Usually deep ruts were the normal condition of the roads, and the motorist simply had to endure them. That is, one endured them so long as the vehicle could hold out against the bumping, jolting, and pounding which the ruts and ridges created.

Henry Ford, in his design for the Model T, went even further than the high wheelers in the attempt to develop an automobile that could negotiate rural America's unpaved roads. Considerably less than half of Americans lived in cities at the turn of the century, and a tremendous market for automobiles existed out there in the country. By building a car that could survive the twisting and jolting of country roads, remain stable, and be able to pull through sticky mud, Ford brought into being a powerful force in the demand for better roads: the Model T-owning farmer who wanted to drive into town on a passable road. A farmer's wife from near Rome, Georgia, wrote to Ford in 1918: "You know, Henry, your car lifted us out of the mud. It brought joy into our lives. We loved every rattle in its bones...."

Model T Ford in deep. North Carolina Division of Archives and History.

Kentucky Historical Society.

**Grading a street with a drag pulled behind the grader to smooth the surface. Ohio Historical Society's Department of Highways Collection.**

Even when roads were dry, it still required considerable horse power, whether mechanical or flesh, to pull a load over them. A 1906 handbook of road engineering compared the force required to move loads over different surfaces:

> In considering the desirability of the different road-surfaces and pavements, it may be noted that a team drawing one ton on a good dirt road can, with the same effort, take two tons over a good macadam surface. Passing from this to a good block-stone pavement, six tons could be drawn as easily, and this load can be increased to eight tons on good wood block or new vitrified brick, or to ten tons on a bituminous macadam or an asphalt pavement.

Maintenance was, and is, a continuing problem, both for the governmental unit whose responsibility it was to keep the roads in good repair and the motorists who had to avoid the chuckholes and endure detours and delays.

As builders brought a road into its final form, both its quality and its longevity seemed to be determined by what happened to the water that fell as precipitation upon it and the surrounding area. Drainage was the single most

Kaimuki. No. 64.

Koau Street Drain.
Aug. 25, 1924.

**Municipal Reference and Records Center, Honolulu, Hawaii.**

**Preparing a trench for a water line across a Tennessee highway. Tennessee State Archives.**

important factor in the design of any new road. It was the subject of countless numbers of speeches at conventions of road engineers and highway officials. Textbooks for the training of new engineers gave it heavy emphasis. The cutting action of flowing water, which bears soil particles, is quite substantial as can be seen in fields and roads following heavy rains. It is particularly obvious in roads proceeding through hilly terrain. Drainage problems even inspired poetry as demonstrated by the following lines printed in the *Topeka Journal* (Kansas) for Dec. 15, 1909.

> On the road to the creaking Water Mill,
> Halting, the mud burdened horses stand still;
> In torrents and gusts pours the pitiless rain
> On the roadway, the builder neglected to drain.
> The driver said: "If I had a boat,
> I could cross this flood,
> But a wagon won't float."

Steam road roller. Tennessee State Archives.

Although, in this instance, the mired vehicle was a wagon, the situation held even more difficulty for the heavier automobile.

The cutting action of narrow wheels, especially metal wheels, carrying heavy loads hastened deterioration of roads. Use of wider tires was proposed as a significant way to keep roads in shape. Further, some persons proposed that use of wider tires should be enforced by law. European drivers commonly used wide tires, and tests conducted by the Missouri Agricultural Experiment Station indicated that wide tires were less wasteful of power than narrow ones. Some persons were so sold on wider tires that they believed their use would do away with ruts and tire-churned mud. But the mud and ruts already were there, "and this fact made the introduction of wider tires extremely difficult, if not impossible. Wide tires, whenever their use was attempted, would wedge in the narrow ruts." The North Carolina legislature passed a bill in 1899, which reduced one's road tax if he used tires of a designated width. The narrow tires at that date were almost exclusively on buggies and wagons; however, the horseless vehicles also performed better when equipped with wider tires. Other values accrued from use of larger tires; in a 1911 advertisement, Oldsmobile claimed that their larger tires contributed to comfort, safety, and economy. "Comfort -- because the tires of a larger circumference literally smooth the way...; absorbing all lesser inequalities and bringing over -- instead of bouncing into -- the larger depressions."

With roads being what they were, the use of rubber tires -- that is, pneumatic rubber tires -- was extremely important in the development of horseless travel, both by bicycle and automobile. Christy Borth referred to the pneumatic tire as "the vehicle's built-in road," and there is no doubt as to the way "high speed" auto travel, 10 to 15 miles per hour perhaps, would feel on early roads if the autos rolled only upon unshod iron wheels. The patent of the pneumatic tire occurred in 1889, which meant that availability of rubber tires blessed the great wave of bicycle production in the United States.

No invention had a more engaging inspiration. In Belfast, Ireland, a Scottish veterinary surgeon, John Boyd Dunlop, watched his young son ride his new bicycle around a cobble-stoned courtyard and decided that the wee bairn would surely shake himself to death on the iron-rimmed wheels. To avoid this catastrophe, the good doctor wrapped pieces of rubber hose around the rims. And so great was the improvement that Dunlop went on to invent the pneumatic tire -- a cushion of air contained in a membrane of rubber.

Photo by U.S. Forest Service.

92

Caufield and Shook Collection, University of Louisville Photographic Archives.

The rubber tire, while aiding the automobilist, may not have been all that much a benefactor to the roads. Ernest Flagg studied European roads and became utterly discouraged with American roads. In his *Roads and Pavements*, he revealed that automobile traffic had a substantially different effect upon road surfaces from that of horse-drawn vehicles. "The tires exert a sucking effect which draws out the particles of the binder from between the stones, and loosens them." He went on to mention other effects of motorized traffic: "At corners and turns in the road the wheels of swiftly moving motor-cars slip and grind the surface, tearing the stones apart and breaking up the crust." Whether or not rubber tires were indeed damaging to highways, particularly gravel and macadam ones, became a question of some controversy. Additional controversy arose over whether or not automobiles did more damage to roads than horse-drawn vehicles. For both classes of vehicles, there was no doubt about the need for improved roads.

One of the most unique ventures in the field of road maintenance occurred in Louisiana during the late 1890s. Obviously, weather is and always has been a great enemy of roads. The kind of weather most damaging in the Deep South was rain, and in Louisiana they had an abundance of it. A planter there determined to build a roof over the road he used between his plantation and the nearest shipping station, a distance of ten miles. He constructed the roof over the road: "It cost him a good deal of money but he paid for it the first year. As you farmers know, it is when the roads are worst that prices are always the best."

**"New Tar, Travel at Your Own Risk." Ohio Historical Society's Department of Highways Collection.**

# 5

# *From Dirt to Rock to Pavement*

**M**otivations for putting a hard surface on roads and streets were many and varied. Early motorists, no doubt, were primary among those who generated the demand for such road improvement. But the wheelmen preceded the automobilists, and teamsters who had sometimes to whip and other times to cajole, as they forced horses and wagons along nearly impossible routes, added their voices to the demand for pavement. Ultimately, the demand became a nationwide roar.

Laying of pavement on the streets of larger cities occurred long before pavement on rural roads. Protection of the dainty shoes of expensively dressed, high society maidens was an important reason for the paving of some city streets. A more unusual motivation led to the paving of Center and Kahler streets in Bucyrus, Ohio, in 1893. A horse-drawn hearse bogged down in the mud and the casket had to be carried down the street through ankle-deep mud by the unfortunate pall bearers. Of course, the factor which finally developed action on the city streets was pure economics; far-sighted business and political leaders simply realized that pavement would pay for itself in increased productivity.

In the highly fertile state of Iowa, the rural-dominated legislature seemed reluctant to put money into pavement. Road construction, yes, but expensive pavement, no. Tradition has it that a change of heart by the legislators occurred on Thanksgiving Day, time of the annual college football classic of the state. Farmers by the thousands drove to the game over the state's excellent dirt roads. During the game a heavy rainstorm turned roads into quagmires of mud. Hundreds of cars mired down and were abandoned, some not to

Give me a little push, please! From the collection of Henry Ford Museum and Greenfield Village.

Street construction on outskirts of Honolulu, 1924. Municipal Reference and Records Center, Honolulu, Hawaii.

**Municipal Reference and Records Center, Honolulu, Hawaii.**

be extricated for days. Thanksgiving dinners went uneaten at many farm homes, and the mood of the state became pro-pavement.

Of course, roads have always been constructed with firm under layers that can support the wearing surface. The quality of that wearing surface, however, was all important because that was the point of interaction between vehicle and road. *Roads and Streets* reported in 1922: "In the mind of the average user of the highways, a road is only as good as its riding surface is smooth... This is true whether the road is earth surfaced, graveled or paved." The feeling about pavement, or at least hard surfaces, was intense as illustrated by the thoughts of engineer William Bruce in 1919:

> No longer will the patient taxpayer be content to see the public moneys spent and almost wasted on merely graded, dirt surfaced roads, with their constant cost of upkeep, but with a loud voice he is now demanding hard-surfaced roads, as good a road to the farm as the cities have in their paved streets.

97

Some of the best of the "improved" hard-surfaced roads of the first two decades of the 20th century were macadam roads. There were very few examples of concrete, brick, or asphalt paving to be seen outside of cities during the first decade, and even by the end of the teens, such pavements were the exception. The crushed-stone macadam roads were of a type commonly employed in Great Britain and continental Europe during the 1800s.

The word "macadam" came from the name of the man who devised the particular technique involved, John Loudon Macadam (or McAdam; both spellings are seen in the literature), in the early 1800s. To build a macadam road, one cuts a shallow roadway, actually just a broad trough, into which crushed rock could be poured and which would hold the rock in position. Usually, this broad trench was twelve or fifteen feet wide and about six inches deep. Then the builders rolled the roadway firmly to compact it, providing a firm foundation and one into which the rock would not penetrate. Next, they spread rock in the trench in three separate layers: an initial layer of rock with the stone

**Building a macadam road -- rolling the broken stone in the background. Tennessee State Archives.**

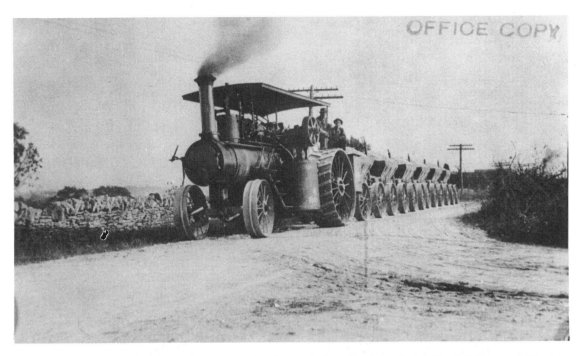

**Group of heavy carts, known as stone boats, carrying broken stone for highway surfacing, pulled by traction engine. Ohio Historical Society's Department of Highways Collection.**

broken into pieces of two to three inches, a middle course broken to sizes between three-quarters to two inches, and an upper, binder layer varying in size from sand to three-quarter-inch pieces and including the dust from the crushing process. They rolled the stone after each layer was applied, packing the stone together. The cementing action of the rock dust resulted in a dense, nearly solid layer of material. They graded a shoulder on each side of the rock road and a ditch adjacent to each shoulder. With a crown in the center of the road tapering to the shoulders, there was good runoff and drainage.

Macadam roads had been maintained for sixty to eighty years in Europe and were highly successful in standing up to traffic of horse-drawn vehicles. The mileage of macadam and other broken stone roads in the United States totaled only about 59,000 miles by the time of the U.S. Office of Inquiry's 1904 road census.

Another type of stone road was the Telford road. First, a Telford builder laid a layer of large stones, eight inches or so in height, carefully by hand, as closely fitted together as possible, upon a graded roadway. Secondly, he spread a layer of broken stone up to about three inches over the large stone and rolled it, then followed it with a layer of sand. Finally, smaller rock was spread, rolled and another layer of sand was added, rolled and watered. The road so constructed was solid, indeed, and adequate for decades of horse-drawn traffic. Because the Telford technique was laborious and expensive, it did not gain as wide acceptance in the United States as it had in Europe.

Initially, such roads were referred to as "broken stone" roads, and later the term "crushed rock" was used. Such usage reflected the manner of preparation of the road-building material. Stone was broken by hand for early roads, but stone crushers powered by steam engines gradually replaced man power. The November 1900 edition of the *Traders' Exchange and Commercial Club News* described operation of a crusher:

> I am sorry that you cannot be out to see the crusher work, but in default of seeing it I will attempt to describe it to you. The stone is fed into a hopper where it is seized between two massive corrugated steel plates and crushed; falling out of the crusher it is taken up by an elevator such as is used for elevating grain,

**Freshly poured curb to the left and broken stone for highway surface. Ohio Historical Society's Department of Highways Collection.**

**Road oil pressure distributor. From Blanchard and Drowne's** *Textbook on Highway Engineering* **published in 1913.**

and dumped into a cylinder about ten feet long and two feet in diameter which is divided into two sections; in one section the cylinder is pierced by holes about an inch in diameter; the cylinder revolves and as it revolves the finer stones and the dust is dropped through the holes into a bin beneath; the larger stones pass to the next division of the cylinder where the holes are larger and the suitably sized stones are in like manner passed through the holes into a bin beneath, while still larger stones finally slip out of the open end of the cylinder into a third bin. These bins are provided with an apron somewhat like a coal chute and from them the stone is loaded into wagons and hauled out upon the road."

The various broken stone roads could be improved by the addition of bituminous binders such as oil, tar and asphalt. In some cases the bitumen was merely poured over the surface of the macadam. In other cases it was rolled and driven into the tiny gaps between the rock fragments, forming what was called bituminous macadam. In still other and rarer cases, the bitumen was mixed thoroughly with the crushed rock prior to spreading and rolling. The latter, of course, was the forerunner of today's asphaltic concrete.

Oil itself, without proper mixture with gravel, sand or crushed rock, was not a good road material. A letter to the editor of the *Horseless Age* in 1905 said:

> Let me sound a note of warning to motor organizations and others interested in the new treatment of road surfaces. Southern California seems to be deluding herself with the impression that oil is a satisfactory substitute for crushed rock and gravel -- and with dire results. Take, for example, the wealthy and prosperous little city of Redlands -- natural soil roads, traffic, dust. Then oil, more oil and still oil. Result, the vilest surface for motoring outside of the pack ice of the polar seas. First make your road of something more substantial than loam -- then oil it.

**Adding oil as a binder for a crushed rock road.**

102

Roads which were categorized as gravel roads comprised considerable variety in style of construction. Sometimes the gravel road actually consisted of little more than an engineered dirt road with gravel spread over the surface. Traffic and the effects of weather moved the gravel down into the road bed, solidifying it and providing traction when the road became wet and sticky. Even into the 1930s, '40s and '50s, the way to travel a gravel road in the spring or after a heavy rain was to "get in them ruts, keep yer foot on the gas, and keep 'er movin' -- there's rock on the bottom that you kin git a grip on." It was a rare occurrence when a Kansas or Missouri farmer got stuck on a gravel road as he traveled in his Model T Ford, but a common occurrence for him to be asked to pull out a city driver. In some other cases, the gravel road was constructed by packing and rolling a road bed, then erecting forms of wood and pouring them full of gravel, much as would be done with poured concrete.

**Ohio Historical Society's Department of Highways Collection.**

**Reworking the surface of a graveled highway. Vermont Historical Society ST-172-7A.**

**Surfacing a city street in Honolulu, 1924. Municipal Reference and Records Center, Honolulu, Hawaii.**

**Loading creek gravel for subsequent road work. Kentucky Historical Society.**

Caufield and Shook Collection, University of Louisville Photographic Archives.

In the early days of gravel roads, road engineers distinguished between gravel, which consisted of smoothed and rounded stones from old river beds, and crushed rock or broken stone, which had rough and irregular surfaces. The broken stone adhered together more firmly, but the smooth stones were easier to work when maintenance was required. The gravel quarriers and road engineers still distinguish between gravel and crushed rock, but on the road, the motorist sees it all as gravel.

Even before the arrival of motor cars and the heavier motor trucks that followed, many paving materials were in place in city business and industrial areas. Wooden blocks, often creosoted and usually cut from southern pine or long-needle pine, were common in the 1880s and '90s. Brick or cut granite blocks were popular paving materials for city thoroughfares and used later to pave intercity highways in some cases. Some cities surfaced streets with macadam or gravel, but such streets didn't stand up well under heavy traffic. The very first pavement in America was a cobblestone street in Pemaquid, Maine,

**Marion County Historical Society.**

**Cutting and laying granite block pavement. From Tobin's *Granite Street Construction* published in 1925.**

laid around 1626. The street was long abandoned and only discovered because a farmer plowing his field ran into an obstruction. Investigation revealed a well-defined, paved street. New York and Boston both had cobble-stone pavements, rounded and smooth stones from about two to six inches in diameter, as early as the mid-1600s.

Brick, cut stone and wooden blocks were most often (and most successfully) laid over a bed of cement-concrete. From this vantage point in time, one wonders why the concrete wasn't sufficient in itself for the final surface. In some instances, the bricks or blocks were placed on a sand base, a procedure adequate only for light traffic and climates where freezing and thawing of the ground didn't "heave" the brick or blocks out of line. Cut stone, particularly granite and quartzite, was used extensively for city curbs and gutters. Very little brick surface appeared in streets prior to 1900; by the time of the 1904

**From Tobin's *Granite Street Construction*.**

**Applying grout between brick pavers.**

**Laying brick pavement in front of a Ford dealership. McClung Collection, Knoxville Public Library.**

**Dearborn Station, Chicago, cut stone pavement. From the collections of Henry Ford Museum and Greenfield Village.**

**Brick pavement without a concrete base was ineffective when the ground underneath heaved with freezing and thawing. From Anderson's *Modern Road Building and Maintenance* published by Hercules Powder Company.**

census, only 123 miles of road were recorded as paved with brick, and most of those miles, some 104, were in the state of Ohio. The first rural road paved with brick was near Cleveland on the Wooster Pike. There, four miles of brick pavement eight feet wide were laid in 1893 between the towns of Parma and Albion. Built at a cost of $10,000 per mile, the right-of-way was sixty feet wide, and the road was carefully engineered, drained and constructed.

The success of that initial brick paving may have been something less than spectacular. Cuyahoga County road engineer James McCleary allegedly said:

> Satisfactory results were achieved slowly and only after many failures in the early road work of the county. He said that the construction of the first brick road in the county was commenced in 1893 and finished in 1895. The wearing surface was 8

ft. in width; tar was used as a filler, and the foundation consisted of 6 ins. of broken stone. No provisions were made for drainage, and there were practically no specifications. Under the action of travel, water and frost the pavement went to pieces, and, as the law under which it was built provided for no expenditure for maintenance -- until the law was amended in 1898, five years after the construction of the pavement -- the chief value of the road, according to Mr. McCleary, was a "horrible example."

Another and altogether novel form of pavement arrived on the scene under arrangements between the Office of Road Inquiry and the Cambria Iron Works of Johnstown, Pennsylvania. *Horseless Age* reported this development in 1897 under the headline, "Steel Highways Being Introduced." Wagon wheels, and later auto wheels, ran in parallel steel tracks, actually shallow troughs eight inches in width. The tracks were placed on a gravel bed and tied together at intervals with steel rod. This roadway provided a very smooth ride and one which required much less locomotive force to travel over, less than 1/12 of that needed for pulling over a macadam road.

Steel rail pavement didn't get very far, and at least one of the drawbacks that defeated it was the fact that they placed two rather than four rails. It must have been difficult to "get on and off" when vehicles passed one another. When "riding the rails" entered the vernacular, it referred only to railroads,

Lower
right hand
corner shows
asphalt block
on concrete
foundation. Next
is about 50ft. brick
laid on clay. Next is
brick on concrete base
The view plainly shows the
failure of brick on a clay
foundation
This view taken by H.J.Kirk
Oct. 15-1918 on South High street
Experimental Road.

Experimenting with road surfaces -- see original notes written in 1918 on the photo. Ohio Historical Society's Department of Highways Collection.

Installing brick road surface. Ohio Historical Society's Department of Highways Collection.

and "hitchhiking" became the term applied to the passenger who sought a free automobile ride.

They tried another form of metallic pavement in New York City in 1865. Cast iron cylinders were placed on end and filled, along with the spaces between, with gravel. Apparently, this pavement wasn't particularly successful either because the city didn't continue with it. It was probably as valuable as the gravel by itself and no more.

Of course, concrete pavement became the favorite of early motorists. It was smooth, level and didn't demand such careful driving attention as other road types. Furthermore, it wore well, required a minimum of maintenance, had no dust problems and was much quieter than other hard-surfaced roads.

**Laying brick pavement in 1919. Kansas State Historical Society.**

Concrete was employed extensively in building construction for basements, foundations, and many other purposes before it became a popular material for road surfacing. The first successful manufacture of Portland cement in the United States was in Coplay, Pennsylvania in 1878, another reason for that year to be specially noted in road history. Concrete was first used for paving in the United States in 1891 when a strip of pavement was laid in front of the courthouse in Bellefontaine, Ohio. It was more than another decade before concrete made it to the country; the first concrete placed on a public rural

A section of the brick paved Midland Trail (later U.S. 60), circa 1920, Kentucky's first federal aid highway construction. Kentucky Historical Society.

road was in Wayne County, Michigan, just outside of Detroit, in 1909. The pavement there was about eighteen feet wide with forty-foot earth shoulders on either side.

The year before the Long Island Motor Parkway Company laid an eleven-mile section of portland-cement concrete, but this was a privately financed venture. It served as a race course for the famous Vanderbilt Cup Races and as a toll parkway and opened Oct. 10, 1908. Likely the first concrete road ever built anywhere, it also was one of the earliest limited-access roads. The highway was twenty-four feet wide, had banked curves and was reinforced by wire mesh, creating a road that had no equal in this country at that time.

In contrast to that broad highway, the first concrete road in the South was a road only nine feet wide. The road stretched westward from Tupelo, Mississippi for some thirteen miles. Construction was started in 1910 and completed in 1913. Further west, Kansas had a concrete road completed late in 1914 from Bassett to Iola. The road extended somewhat over one mile, was eighteen feet wide with four-foot macadam shoulders, and cost $10,000 for the project. The first use of reinforced concrete for public highway construction was in New Jersey in 1912, on what became state route 24.

Concrete Street, Meridian Place, Washington, D. C., Built With
OLD DOMINION PORTLAND CEMENT

The roads mentioned above were all cast-in-place, but a Wyoming group tried pre-cast concrete for a road built in 1920. Slabs of concrete nine feet wide comprised the experimental section. They were placed upon a cushion of sand over a sub-grade constructed as for a traditional monolithic concrete pavement. Teams of horses hauled the pre-cast slabs into position. Although there was only 2400 feet of this pavement, it appeared to wear well during its first year, even though exposed to heavy oil field traffic.

Perhaps the greatest stimulus toward widespread use of concrete

Concrete paved highway typical of the 1920s and '30s. Library of Congress.

Monument commemorating first concrete street pavement in Bellefountaine, Ohio, in 1891.

Paving with concrete, 1920s style. Portland Cement Association, Skokie, Illinois.

Constructing curbs and gutters, paving with concrete, and installing streetcar tracks on King Street, Honolulu. Municipal Reference and Records Center, Honolulu, Hawaii.

**Concrete paving -- installation of forms. Ohio Historical Society's Department of Highways Collection.**

was the construction of "seedling" sections of concrete highway along the route of the historic Lincoln Highway. These sections were a single mile in length, constructed from cement contributed by the member companies of the Portland Cement Association. It was originally intended that "seedling" miles would be built by local groups in the six states between Chicago and California along the proposed route of the highway. The first mile was built near DeKalb, Illinois, in 1914, and the second near Grand Island, Nebraska, was completed in November 1915. The "seedlings" provided a national object lesson in quality of road surface. The action of the Lincoln Highway Association, in publicizing these outstanding sections of highway, did much to educate Americans about the potential for rapid and efficient travel by automobile.

One of the most unusual highway projects of the teens and early '20s occurred in Delaware. One of the members of that state's first highway department, T. Coleman duPont, personally financed the construction, including purchase of right-of-way, of duPont Boulevard and gave it to the state. The highway extended from the Maryland state boundary to the city of Wilmington, a distance of some 96.7 miles. He originally proposed it in 1912, and the highway was complete ten years later in 1922. The recorded cost to builder duPont was nearly $4 million, an amount which compared favorably with what some individual states were spending during the teens for highway construction during a whole year.

**Concrete paving project in 1918 in Colorado. Denver Public Library, Western History Collection.**

Another historic project was the "Ideal Section" of the Lincoln Highway, constructed in 1922 on the Illinois-Indiana state line about thirty miles south of Chicago. After consultation with the leading highway engineers of the day, Lincoln Highway officials developed specifications for a road which was to be an "ultimate" highway. Pavement was concrete, forty feet wide, on a right-of-way 110 feet wide. The forty feet allowed for four traffic lanes, and the 110 feet provided room for pedestrian side paths, utility lines and landscaping. The design was intended to allow for automobiles traveling at an average speed of thirty-five miles per hour; trucks were expected to average ten miles per hour. Unfortunately, the ideal highway was only a mile and a third long. However, it did serve as an effective model of what was needed by the nation for handling the traffic soon to be generated by the "travelingest" people in history.

A number of model roads or object-lesson roads had been built earlier. One of the initial projects carried out by the Office of Road Inquiry was an object-lesson road constructed at the site of the New Jersey Agricultural College and Experiment Station in 1897. It was a short piece of improved road, only 660 feet. They dressed the roadbed to appropriate shape and surfaced it with crushed stone to a width of eight feet and a depth of six inches. Director of the Office, General Roy Stone, complimented the project: "This method is especially valuable in teaching the importance of good roads and the possibility of obtaining them."

Between 1904 and 1906, the Office of Road Inquiry participated in the building of no less than thirty-six object-lesson roads. The office required the local community or county where the road was located to pay for right-of-way, labor, materials and animal power, and provided the engineering advice, surveys, supervision, and road machinery. The roads featured different materials -- shells at Fernandina, Florida, and Beaumont, Texas; granite and brick in Columbus, Ohio, and Bellingham, Washington; and sand-clay roads in North Carolina. Most of those built elsewhere were of gravel or crushed rock.

Roads constructed by wealthy individuals on the grounds of their estates provided other object-lesson roads. The Biltmore Estate of Cornelius Vanderbilt near Asheville, North Carolina, had model drives. Good roads enthusiasts of that city organized the Good Roads Association of Asheville and Buncombe County in 1899, and that group raised $5000 by private subscription to build a macadam road between the city and the estate's good roads.

Asphalt was another surfacing material which provided a smooth as well as durable pavement. The early source of asphalt was natural deposits, particularly a large "lake" of asphalt on the Caribbean island of Trinidad. Probably the very first use of asphalt for street paving was in Newark, New Jersey, in 1870, and then New York City tried asphalt in 1871. Today most asphalt is obtained as a distillation product from crude oil. But the first substantial use of this petroleum-based and semi-solid material (liquid when hot and solid when cool) was in Washington, D.C. The years 1877 and 1878 again are significant in the history of automobile highways. It was in those years that Amzi Lorenzo Barber obtained a franchise to remove asphalt from the Trinidad deposits and began to use it to pave the streets of the nation's capital. Barber's work actually was the first extensive production of what we might call a modern pavement in the United States.

Although Washington perhaps should have been America's "showcase" city and, in terms of architectural quality may have been, in streets and boulevards prior to 1880 it was a disaster. Streets were loblollies and often bordered on the impassable. But during the 1880s, the city began to build streets equivalent to her beautiful government buildings and, thanks to Barber, began to look the part of the capital city of a progressive, wealthy nation. Buffalo, New York, and other cities soon followed suit. Asphaltic pavements comprised of ten percent to fifteen percent asphalt, holding together an aggregate of gravel or crushed rock and better known as "blacktop," became the country's most widely used paving materials.

Laying asphalt paving by hand prior to "hot mix" machines. Caufield and Shook Collection, University of Louisville Photographic Archives.

124

Asphalt paving project. The roller in the background is ready to smooth the surface. Caufield and Shook Collection, University of Louisville Photographic Archives.

During early years of its usage, asphalt also was laid in block form. The blocks were somewhat larger than brick and laid upon a gravel or concrete base. Made with a hydraulic press, the blocks were very dense and resistant to wear and were used in areas of heavy traffic. Most of asphalt block pavement, because of its expense, appeared on city streets rather than in rural areas.

Molasses was not as successful when used as a paving material. Yes, in 1908 near Newton, Massachusetts, the molasses refuse from a sugar refinery was combined with lime and then used as a road binder. The road so constructed sustained traffic for several years, but the method was judged impractical because of cost and the material's solubility in water.

**Major city street in Honolulu, 1920. Municipal Reference and Records Center, Honolulu, Hawaii.**

All varieties of roads deteriorate with time, effects of weather, and especially with the wear of traffic. An early technique employed to reduce deterioration by traffic was dual surfacing; half of a road had a macadam surface and half a dirt surface. The intention was for the dirt or clay surface to be used in dry weather, leaving the macadam to be used as needed in wet weather. As long as the clay surface remained smooth, the idea worked. But when ruts and holes developed in the dirt lane, motorists abandoned it and drove upon the smoother macadam, regardless of weather conditions. Similar single lane pavements or "half roads" combined a dirt or clay lane with brick or concrete. An article in *The Literary Digest* as late as 1931 advocated the practice:

> It is as foolish to build a twenty-foot road where a ten-foot one would do, as it would be to try to get along with the narrower one in heavy traffic. Best of all, halving the width doubles the length without extra cost; and in many rural regions, length, rather than width, is what is needed.

And at that time Missouri already had 420 miles of single-lane pavement, and in 1929, a single Maryland county built fifty-one miles of such rural pavement.

Regardless of the type of pavement, a good road, even when defined in 1900, was "a permanent road -- a road that is hard and smooth, and fit for service at all seasons of the year." Add to that a reasonable price, ease of maintenance,

**Delivery of cut stone for curbs on a city street. From Tobin's *Granite Street Construction* published in 1925.**

and durability, and one has the characteristics sought in all varieties of road. In all cases, it took a good deal of "trial and error" before the best techniques for building that "good" road were perfected. A North Carolina highway official wrote in 1924, "After three years I am amazed at how little we knew about building roads in North Carolina in 1921." And if that was true in '21, how much truer it was in the earlier years as engineers, contractors and volunteers tried to find methods to build good and lasting roads.

# What Shall We Do With Our Dirt Roads?

Make permanent highways out of them as fast as possible—but, eighty per cent of our public roads are of the dirt variety, and it will take years to transform even a part of this immense mileage into hard roads. In the meantime we must maintain our dirt roads in the best possible state in the only possible way—

## USE ROAD MACHINES AND ROAD DRAGS

The Big Winner Reversible Road Machine
For Use With Horse or Engine Power

### The Winner Line of Road Machines

includes the Little Winner, a 6 ft. Blade, 1600 pound machine; the Standard Winner, a 7 ft. Blade, 2500 pound machine; the Big Winner, an 8 ft. Blade, 3500 pound machine; the Giant Winner, a 10 ft. Blade, 5500 pound machine; and the Giant Winner, a 12 ft. Blade, 7000 pound machine. One of these machines will just fit your needs. Write us about your work and we will recommend the machine you should have.

### The Champion Two-Blade Road Drag

With independently adjustable blades is the Road Drag above all others that suits average conditions of dragging. Weight 280 lbs. Can be used with two or three horses. Blades 7 feet six inches long, 6 inches wide. Reasonable in price, with practically no cost for upkeep this is the Road Drag that will suit you.

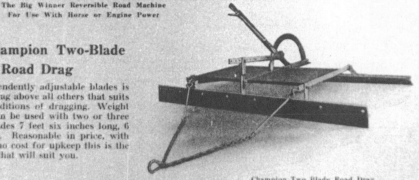

Champion Two Blade Road Drag

### The York State Hone

is the most complete Hone or Drag on the market. With this implement it is possible to smooth, crown and puddle earth roads. This machine is 10 ft. long, 5½ ft. wide and 8 inches high.

The York State Road Hone

You should have our complete catalogue, "Everything for the Roadmaker." It is free for the asking.

# The Good Roads Machinery Company
## KENNETT SQUARE, PA.

A mysterious power
seems to help them to go,
Through sand, mud and water, o'er
mountain and snow
-- *Ford Times*, 1913

Helpful Highwaymen

There's an all-sufficient reason
For the crowd that's here today,
They are boosters, and are boosting
For an inter-state highway.

They're a band of bold highwaymen,
Wearing Cleopatra smiles,
And their civic hallelujahs
May be heard a hundred miles.

Every mother's son among them
Brought his brains and lungs along,
And will boost for this great highway
In a voice that's clear and strong.
-- *Topeka Capital*, Dec. 3, 1911

# 6
# *Muscle Power to Machine Power*

**E**arly road building involved, of course, a great deal of manual labor. Road construction always required that much earth be moved, even at the very beginning. Road beds had to be packed and solidified, and surfacing materials prepared and added.

A number of different kinds of equipment were available, but power for their movement usually came from horse or mule, sometimes from a steam or gasoline traction engine and, of course, often from the strong backs of men. Early in the century, the strong backs were those who "worked out" their road tax. Later, the strong backs were those of convicts brought from prison to work on roads or highways.

Even after machines became dominant, labor in road construction continued to be grueling. Men worked hard operating those machines, controlling horses and mules that powered them, or maneuvering huge steam or gasoline traction engines. Muscle power rather than hydraulic power moved grader blades to new heights or angles. Muscle power dumped the earth out of scrapers. James Morris even suggested that, "By and large, the difference between a rich nation and a poor one is the difference between a mechanized and...a muscular society." Whether or not the United States was a rich nation in 1900, the development of highways, and the trucks and automobiles which traveled them, certainly paralleled and contributed to making the nation much richer than it was. Road building during the early years of the century featured muscle power and very simple machinery, and, of course, not many miles of road were completed. The years 1910 to 1925 witnessed the conversion from muscle power to mechanical power for road building; output, thereafter, increased every year.

After purchase or other establishment of right-of-way for a new road, the roadway had to be cleared of everything from weeds and brush to large trees and boulders. Frost's *The Art of Roadmaking* lists the following tools needed for "clearing and grubbing: bush hooks, axes, grub hoes, mattocks, stump-pulling machine and cross cut saws," as well as these necessary "tools for grading: picks, grading pick, clay pick, shovels, ploughs, wheelbarrows, scrapers." These lists emphasize the fact that early road making was "by hand." Of note was the fact that "The maximum distance to which earth can be wheeled economically in barrows is about 200 feet." Most of us would hate to move dirt that far in a wheelbarrow, regardless of whether it was economical or not. A later report on roads and roadbuilding materials from the Georgia Geological Survey

**Dump scraper, one mule or horse, and one man.**

listed these "tools and machines used in highway construction: plows, road scrapers, road machines, road rollers, rock-crushers and wagons," indicative of a more developed methodology for road making, involving machines.

For changing the grade of a roadway or "the lay of the land," the surface was plowed and scrapers of several varieties moved the loosened material.

> In operating a drag scraper, it is usually drawn by one or two horses. To load, a man grasps the handles and pushes the cutting edge down into the loosened earth as the scraper is pulled along. Then the full scraper is dragged along on its bottom to the point of dump, where either the driver or a dump man takes hold of one or both of the handles and lifts the scraper so that it turns upside down about its cutting edge.

Wheeled scrapers could handle larger loads and were essentially a drag scraper mounted on wheels with substantial levers for raising, lowering and

FIG. 103.—Wheel Scraper.

**Wheel scraper. From Frost's *The Art of Roadmaking*.**

dumping. Another important machine was the Fresno Grader or buck scraper. More easily loaded and capable of carrying a larger load than a drag scraper, it usually was pulled by four horses. The name was derived from the city of origin, Fresno, California, and fresnos were used primarily in construction in the West.

Later, much of the work accomplished earlier with scrapers was done with the larger road graders, also known as road scrapers, road machines or road hones. These road machines were described rather well by the same Georgia Geological Survey publication:

> They are all made upon the same plan, differing only in detail of construction. They consist of a large iron or steel scraper, mounted on wheels, so attached to a suspended frame as to be easily adjusted at any angle, by the movement of certain levers.
>
> A good road-machine will do the work of twenty laborers; and when put to its best will do the work of forty.... Anyone, who has compared the road built by the old-fashioned method with its rough, uneven surface, with the clean ditches and smooth and even surface of a road built by the machine method by a good

**Advanced Fresno scraper. New Mexico Highway Department.**

operator, will not hesitate long in passing judgment on the two methods.

The effectiveness and utility of road machines is corroborated in all sorts of road construction documents. The following is certainly typical:

A large part of the earth roads now built or reconstructed, especially those in the prairie states, are made with road machines. These are built in many sizes for both horse and tractor hauling, and serve a variety of purposes in an economical manner. They are not adapted for making cuts and fills, although frequently employed in shaping a road after the grading has been done.

If the work is on a scale large enough to warrant the use of two graders hauled by a tractor, a trained grading crew is often able to build a good roadbed at very low cost. Mechanical traction has resulted in the development of methods of construction impracticable when teams of four to eight horses were employed, and as a general proposition mechanical traction is most economical....

A specialized variety of grader -- the elevating grader or "new era" grader -- had wide usage for many years. It not only could grade newly loosened dirt, it could pick it up and dump it in piles or wagons. Initially, several teams of horses or mules pulled this type of grader; later, steam or gasoline traction engines pulled them. An elevating grader consisted of a tall grader frame, an elevator similar to what farmers used for grain, and a chute out of which the dirt was dumped into wagons or piled in windrows. The Georgia Geological Survey was dubious about the value of this kind of road implement: "This class of machine is rather complicated; and it will probably never come into general use on ordinary country roads."

Steam road roller in action on Clarksville, Tennessee street. Clarksville/Montgomery County Museum.

Another important device used for loosening and moving earth was the scarifier. It was a modified and especially heavy, tough plow used primarily in the reworking of existing roads rather than in making new ones. Some scarifiers were constructed with the same frame as a road grader but with the blade replaced by a heavy toothed plow. In other cases, the plow units were attached to a grader or to a motorized roller. The earliest scarifiers were separate units, very heavy, and were towed by horses or mules.

The grade of a highway generally followed the hills and valleys over which it was built. Although road

**Russell Elevating Grader. Kansas Historical Society.**

**Elevating grader. New Mexico Highway Department.**

**Road roller equipped with scarifiers.**

construction did not require the extreme flatness needed in railroad construction, the trend from the beginning was toward more and more alteration of topography, deeper cuts and larger fills. Early in the century, steam shovels accomplished major earth movements only to be replaced by bulldozers, draglines and earth-movers during the 1920s and 1930s.

Horse-drawn dump wagons moved quantities of earth from cut to fill. Some of the dump wagons were used individually, but in other cases, trains of dump wagons were pulled by steam traction engines.

One of the major manufacturers of dump wagons was the Eagle Wagon Works of Auburn, New York. Initially a Syracuse firm, the company held a number of important patents related to dump-bottom wagons, and their product was in popular demand:

Road roller equipped with scarifiers.

**Denver Public Library, Western History Collection.**

Not only large cities, but the good road movement, has made a large demand for the Eagle Dump Wagons, they being used in team work for grading and hauling, and also in traction train hauls when crushed stone, gravel or other material is placed upon the road bed.

Other major wagon makers included the Tiffin Wagon Company of Tiffin, Ohio, and Stroud and Company, who manufactured "Little Red" dump wagons in Omaha.

Of course, as soon as motor trucks developed to the point that they could carry heavy loads and negotiate the rough terrain of road construction sites, they were employed extensively in construction.

In road work, more than in many other kinds of contract work, the item of transporting material -- and to a lesser extent, men and equipment -- to and from the work, and hauling material on the work itself, forms a large part of the cost of construction. This is especially true in work on country roads situated at a considerable distance from sources of supply... or on work involving heavy grading where it is necessary to move large quantities of earth or rock... before contracting was conducted with the same intelligence and skill as are brought to bear upon the conduct of other lines of business, the two-wheeled, horse-drawn cart and the stone boat furnished the principal means of hauling. In time these were replaced by four-wheeled, horse-drawn dump wagons of varying capacities.... Within the past few years another means of transportation -- the motor truck -- has come into use, and when substituted for horse-drawn equipment has proven efficient and economical for many kinds of work.

While hauling was the most significant role played by trucks, some trucks were outfitted with blades and used for grading or snow plowing. Others towed drags or road machines or were equipped with tanks and distributors for oil or water. Studies as early as 1913 indicated that motorized hauling could beat the cost of horse-drawn hauling by a wide margin. The great transition to trucks, however, didn't occur until World War I. Trucks contributed extensively to the U.S. Army in Europe, and a tremendous number of trucks were "left over" at the end of the war. The Army returned these to the United States, and the federal government distributed them to the state highway departments for use in road construction. Contractors followed the highway departments rather quickly in the exchange of animal horse power for motorized

141

**From Hercules Powder Company's** *Modern Road Building and Maintenance.*

**Sand or stone-chip distributor, drawn by a team of horses or mules.**

horse power. Gasoline was easier to handle than oats and hay, and trucks did not leave any messy deposits in the way. England and England, a Minnesota and Dakota contracting company "changed from horse-drawn equipment to the new modern Ford dump trucks and caterpillar tractors and blading equipment." The machinery replaced was described by one of the England children:

> The road grading equipment used in the early days of road grading was, of course, horse-drawn. They used both horses and mules for the equipment, graders, dump-wagons, and blades. As many teams were used as were necessary to pull the load. Usually, the dump wagons used one team of mules, while the other equipment used from one to three or four teams, depending on conditions due to weather and soil. They used two large canvas circus tents for the stables with pole stalls and metal feed bunks that could be easily set up after each move.

**Sandusky tractor. The R.B. Hayes Presidential Center, Charles E. Frohman Collection.**

After most contractors were mechanized, the investment required to get started in road construction was substantial, or as characterized by a well-known Massachusetts contractor, "enormously large in proportion to the amount of work done per year." Earlier, when road building first began to be a common enough process and sufficiently profitable to attract people into establishing road contracting businesses, it required little capital to begin. The necessary start-up equipment comprised some hand tools and perhaps a single road machine and roller. The most expensive part of the contractor's investment was for two or three teams of horses.

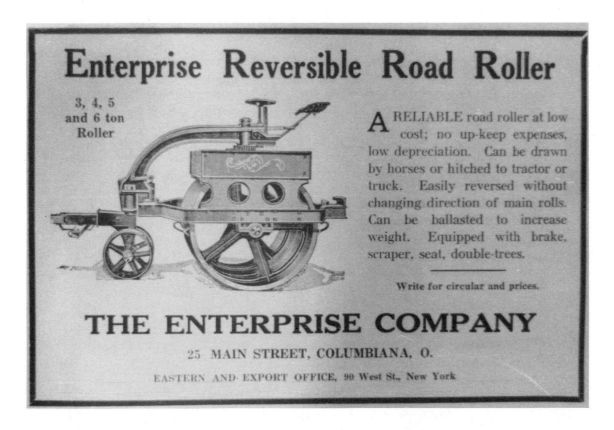

Compaction of a roadbed initially was accomplished as a by-product of other parts of the construction process. Iron wheels of wagons or graders and animal hooves did much of it. Wagons deliberately were built with front and rear axles of different length so that wheels did not "track" and a wider swath of earth could be packed with a single pass of the wagon. Horse-drawn rollers were common, obviously of smaller size and lighter weight than the steam or gasoline rollers that replaced them. Most of the horse-drawn rollers were so constructed that they could be pulled from either direction, allowing for unhitching the team that pulled it and rehitching for pulling in the opposite direction. This allowed a tremendous saving in time and equine energy over the large semicircular pathway which would have been required to turn around a roller.

More effective than smooth rollers for compacting fresh earth were tamping rollers or rolling tampers, rollers with what appeared to be feet on them. The device was invented by John Fitzgerald of California:

> ... he was led to invent the rolling tamper by seeing the effect that a flock of sheep produced upon a road that he was building. He had just plowed the road, and was about to crown it up with a road machine when a flock of about 10,000 sheep came along. The feet of the first sheep sank deep into the plowed soil, but the feet of the next sheep walked upon the surface of the soil which had been beaten into a mass as hard as brick by the feet of the sheep ahead. Fitzgerald said: "You can well believe I was the maddest man in Kern county when I had to break up that crust and found that even a pick pointed plow would scarcely faze it.

**TrucTracTor pulling multiple "sheep foot" rollers for compacting a road bed.**

He remarked to his partner that, if the sheep had waited only a few hours, until the road had been properly crowned, he would have paid good money to have had them walk over the road and compact it.

"A thought then struck me," said Fitzgerald. "I couldn't afford to hire a flock of sheep. Why not invent a flock?"

And he did, for his rolling tamper is a mechanical flock of sheep.

The old split-log drag proved effective for maintaining earth roads, it was inexpensive, and anyone could construct one. It was not long, however, before tinkerers were trying to make drags that were stronger and more durable. A number of companies began to manufacture drags constructed of steel. However, many of the older road workers refused to use the new-fangled metal drags, swearing that the old-fashioned split log was more effective. And, of course, as both users and manufacturers experimented with drags, they also began to experiment with and to build other simple road machinery.

For many of these early companies, the road machinery was strictly a sideline. Many were farm implement companies such as J.I. Case, Hart-Parr, Huber, John Deere and Company, New Holland, and International Harvester. By the mid '30s, Huber was really a road machinery company, but J.I. Case and John Deere successfully straddled the fence between road and field.

One of the major companies in the manufacture and sale of road graders was the J.D. Adams Company, unique in that it was started for the sole purpose of making a better road grader. It remained a manufacturer of road grading machinery throughout its existence. Also, it was one of the real pioneers of the industry, dating back to 1885. Joseph D. Adams was a farmer and country school teacher in west-central Indiana. He was elected by his fellow citizens to the office of district road supervisor, even though he did not aspire to or run for that office. As supervisor, Adams surprised his constituents by insisting on as much quality in their labor when they "worked out the road tax" as they put into their own farm work. Adams was totally inexperienced in road work, but he took his responsibility seriously. In his learning about road construction and maintenance, he soon discovered the inadequacy of road making equipment. He then became an agent to sell road machinery, traveling Indiana and nearby states, and as he interviewed supervisors and county commissioners, he absorbed a wealth of information about what was needed to build roads more easily and efficiently. In 1879, young Adams first worked with a wagon-type grader and found it ineffective. Six years later, in 1885, Adams put together his own grader, a revolutionary machine because the wheels could be tilted. The "leaning wheel" grader allowed for operation along

148

a slope such as the ditch beside a road. Weight of a grader tended to cause it to slip down a slope. Straight wheel graders would skid out of line as they attempted to move a layer of earth. Leaning wheels allowed the front of the grader to stand upright and "lean in" to the dirt load.

The leaning wheel concept put Adams way ahead of his competitors, and this feature was eventually incorporated into the road machines of all manufacturers. Adams made significant developments in grader construction. One was a steerable tongue that allowed for steering the grader independently of the team or traction engine pulling it. Another was the introduction of blades considerably wider than the machine proper, even up to twelve feet, as early as 1905.

As in the development of the automobile industry, manufacturers of the early primitive road construction machinery sprang up all over the place. In a fashion similar to the many individuals and companies that tried to make it as automobile manufacturers, many companies tried to build road machinery of one sort or another. If, however, we think of such cities as Springfield, Massachusetts; Kokomo, Indiana; Detroit; and Cleveland as primary cradles for the developing automotive industry, then the developing road machinery industry likewise was cradled in Indianapolis, Peoria, Minneapolis and, perhaps most importantly, in Ohio.

In 1913, the National Association of Road Material and Machinery Manufacturers numbered eighty-six members. Nearly twenty percent of them were Ohio firms; only New York had more, and a number of those firms were merely agents who imported European equipment.

The small city of Marion had a substantial impact on road construction in central Ohio, giving rise to the Huber Manufacturing Company, Marion Steam Shovel Company, Fairbanks Steam Shovel Company and Ohio Tractor Manufacturing Company. Just a few miles to the east was the town of Galion, where the Galion Iron Works devel-

**Early offices of the Galion Iron Works, Galion, Ohio, with the F.W. Woolworth store downstairs. Galion Manufacturing Division, Dresser Industries, Inc.**

oped. Galion began business in 1907 as a foundry and machine shop manufacturing culvert pipe. They cast large culverts of iron, made in halves which were then bolted together in place as roads, driveways or railroads were constructed over them. While still a small company, Galion experimented with, built, and marketed a wide variety of road and other construction equipment, beginning, of course, with a simple road drag.

Back in Marion, Edward Huber and Lewis Gunn formed a partnership in 1863 to manufacture farm implements designed and patented by Huber. Of special note is a revolving hay rake. Huber also invented and patented a steam-powered farm engine and a grain thresher. In 1874, they incorporated the Huber Manufacturing Company to carry on the business of manufacturing and selling steam traction engines, portable and stationary engines, grain

Testing room, with steam road rollers, in the Huber factory. Marion County Historical Society.

threshers and the revolving hay rake, which was their first successful product.

During the 1880s, the company entered the road construction equipment business, although company officials would have been surprised to hear anyone say so. During 1883, Huber manufactured about 2,000 revolving steel scrapers and 3000 steel dump scrapers in addition to 150 engines, 150 threshers and 6000 hay rakes. Probably few purchasers of those scrapers and dump scrapers bought them with the intent that they would be used primarily for road work. Some were purchased by building contractors and the majority by farmers, but some, no doubt, were used in road projects.

The company announced in 1894 the Huber "Gasoline Traction Engine -- a new development in farm power," which was to replace the steam engine in powering threshing machines. Huber is generally credited with being first to put gas tractor production on a commercial basis. Some of these lumbering giants and their brothers, the steam traction engines, found their way into road construction to pull heavy loads of gravel or broken stone for macadam. Still, a description of the company in 1907 gave no hint of the road business and claimed that "the company has built up the largest exclusive threshing machine factory in the world."

The deliberate entry of Huber into the road machinery field came only a year later in 1908 when it introduced a steam road roller. These machines really were steam traction engines with a heavy roll taking the place of the front wheels and with the rear wheels made extra wide. Huber followed in 1923 with its "Automotive Type Motor Roller," which the company claimed "revolutionized the road construction industry here and abroad...every roller in the world became obsolete the instant Huber announced its new model." Indeed, the

**Huber road roller pulling Russell grader. Marion County Historical Society.**

Huber road roller. Marion County Historical society.

Machine shop in the Huber factory. Marion County Historical Society.

# The HUBER Manufacturing Co.

**RoadTools** ROLLERS MAINTAINERS TRACTORS

MARION, OHIO. U.S.A.

Every mile of *rough, rutted, chuck-holed road* under your jurisdiction is there with your full permission and consent.

If you will take two minutes to read this letter and spend a little additional time looking over the circular, you will be convinced that almost impassable roads as found in some localities are altogether unnecessary and uncalled for.

Hundreds of miles of roads, as bad or worse than yours, have been transformed into highways capable of carrying heavy traffic the year 'round, by one man on a HUBER POWER MAINTAINER. Not only do earth roads yield to its treatment, but it is particularly effective on worn out, or partly worn out gravel or macadam. The powerful scarifier will dig through the high places; the end of the flexible blade will dip down and reclaim material that has been scattered and spread and the diagonal cutting blade, set at the proper angle and hung midway the long wheel base, levels the job and leaves it smooth—*and one man does it all.*

In addition to rebuilding your old roads and making them passable, the HUBER MAINTAINER will keep your good roads in first class condition and prolong their life indefinitely, saving the cost of expensive repairs.

What is this HUBER MAINTAINER? How does it differ from other maintainers?

The HUBER MAINTAINER is a *big* machine—and a heavy one. Look at the cut in the folder. The drive wheels are five feet high; its total length is more than 16 feet; the blade is 12 feet long and the outfit weighs more than 9,000 pounds, with weight properly distributed to hold the blade on the ground.

And it has the power—surplus power—to pull through, even in the heaviest cutting and when the scarifier is down to the bar. If the side ditch is very deep you can not get into it with any self contained maintainer, but the Huber is the only maintainer that has sufficient draw bar power to pull a detached grader for cleaning out deep ditches—it developes practically 20 h. p. on the draw bar—more than many road tractors.

The Huber Maintainer is *built to last* and to operate *without breakage*. The blade beams are real plow beam stock, full size, two to each blade section. The outrigging is heavy angle iron braced against all strains. The frame is double trussed and all other parts including bolts, rivets, shafts and springs are greatly oversize. There is no weak point in the HUBER MAINTAINER.

You should be intensely interested in this machine. You should ask us to send additional proof of the statements we make. Or, better yet, let us show you on your own roads just what the HUBER MAINTAINER will do and the time and money it will save. You can't lose—it must perform as we say or you haven't bought a thing.

Please return the card—today. It places you under no obligation and it puts it up to us to show you *we mean business.*

THE HUBER MANUFACTURING COMPANY
MARION, OHIO

appearance of rollers has not changed appreciably in the succeeding fifty-six years.

Huber introduced a one-man Maintainer in 1920. It was basically an extended version of the company's farm tractor, from which a flexible grader was suspended. Huber also constructed heavy graders to be pulled by traction engines or other vehicles from 1921 on.

Also located in the city of Marion was the Marion Steam Shovel Company, incorporated in 1884. Marion shovels figured materially in the construction of every major railroad constructed in the late 19th and early years of the 20th centuries. When road and highway construction began to include "cuts" and "fills" similar to preparation of railroad beds, Marion shovels played an important role.

The Galion Iron Works never manufactured tractors, plows, threshing machines, or other agricultural implements. From its early days, Galion built horse-drawn scrapers, sprinkling wagons, gravel spreaders, rock crushers, gravel sorting plants, gravel and rock moving equipment, coal-loading equipment, belt conveyors, and dredges. The company sold some of their products through jobbers and some directly to users. Most items were made to order during the early years of operation. By 1911, Galion had designed and begun production of its own horse-drawn road grader. It was small by today's standards: about fifteen feet long and a little taller than a man, was light enough to be pulled by two horses, and a single operator stood at the rear of the grader. Machines of this type found use in construction of the vast majority of roads built during the 'teens, a time of great demand for roads by automobilists and their organizations, yet before extensive federal involvement in funding.

In 1913, the company changed its name to Galion Iron Works and Manufacturing, and then in 1915 produced a really sophisticated grader, "The Galion Light Premier." The grader was featured as light enough to be pulled by two horses yet strong enough for four. Its moldboard was six feet, six inches long and, in addition to raising and lowering, the blade could be turned, slanted and even shifted sideways. The machine was so well accepted that it remained in production long past the advent of self-propelled graders, all the way up to 1945.

Galion people watched as the power and dependability of the internal combustion engine improved and, in 1922, proceeded with development of a heavy-duty, self-propelled grader. A tractor engine located in the rear of the grader frame provided driving power to the rear wheels. The moldboard was in the center, and above it were the machine's controls and a position where the operator could stand behind them. The motorized grader evolved rapidly for

**Huber Maintainer in action, circa 1924. Marion County Historical Society.**

New Mexico Highway Department.

**Portable gravel screening plant. Galion Manufacturing Division, Dresser Industries, Inc.**

Advertisement for the portable gravel plant, pictured above. *Good Roads* magazine, 1919.

**Illustration of the Galion Light Premier grader. Galion Manufacturing Division, Dresser Industries, Inc.**

Galion during the '20s, and the familiar yellow Galion machines began to cover the United States and the world.

Road rollers joined the Galion line during the early '20s, and, subsequently, the company became the world's largest roller manufacturer. Galion built its first experimental roller during 1916 and 1917, and completed its first production model in March 1921. Huge two-cylinder gasoline engines with enormous flywheels provided power but were exceedingly hard to get started. Galion then turned to steam, a motive force that Huber had employed extensively but which Galion had largely ignored. In 1922, Galion introduced its first steam roller, a three-wheeled type which, in appearance, resembled a standard steam tractor with front wheels replaced by a heavy roll.

A major change came in 1924 with introduction of the Galion Little Master roller. This machine was less bulky and genuinely easy to handle. No longer a "monster machine," it was powered by a Fordson tractor engine, basically the old Model T Ford engine that was so simple and efficient it already had revolu-

The first motorized grader made by Galion and probably the first motor grader built, circa 1911; actually a modified horse-drawn Light Premier grader. Galion Manufacturing Division, Dresser Industries, Inc.

Illustration prepared for Galion advertising. Galion Manufacturing Division, Dresser Industries, Inc.

Twelve-foot leaning-wheel pulled grader, circa 1924. Galion Manufacturing, Dresser Industries, Inc.

Galion Manufacturing Division, Dresser Industries, Inc.

An early gasoline-powered road roller equipped with grader blade.

Galion Master road roller. Galion Manufacturing Division, Dresser Industries, Inc.

tionized both the automobile industry and, subsequently, the farm tractor industry. From the 1920s on, Galion was a major industry, and the primary builder of many types of road construction equipment.

The giant of them all among road equipment makers, the Caterpillar Tractor Company of Peoria, Illinois, also had an agricultural beginning but soon deserted it, and throughout the company's life has been devoted to manufacturing equipment for the "dirt-moving" industry. Caterpillar originated in a rich but unusual agricultural environment in California's San Joaquin Valley. Soil in the valley was fertile but very soft, and horses' hooves and tractor wheels sank deep in the dirt.

As a manufacturer of steam traction engines, Benjamin Holt tried to find ways to make his heavy machines functional in the valley's soft soil. He tried to spread the great weight of the tractor over a larger number of wide drive wheels, finally outfitting one of his tractors with six drive wheels, each six feet wide, making a tractor nearly forty-six feet wide. Then a better idea came to Holt, a machine which could lay out its own road as it proceeded and pick it back up after going by. He removed the rear wheels of a tractor and replaced them with treadmills, that is, with continuous chains of wooden blocks or shoes. Testing of his first practical crawler tractor took place on Nov. 24, 1904; it worked. Although the idea was not new, Holt was the first to make it work.

Holt's steam crawler tractor was still a huge, unwieldy monster, but the switch from steam to gasoline power allowed for shrinking the size of the machine. Subsequent design changes left the crawler resembling the modern "bulldozer." The first production crawler using gasoline for power sold in 1908, and, thereafter, business boomed. By 1915, there were over 2000 Holt crawlers in use in over twenty countries.

The history of Caterpillar includes a set of similar developments just a few miles west in San Leandro, California. There, Daniel Best also made huge steam tractors, and, likewise, his tractors sank into the soft soil. Best, too, was an ingenious person and outfitted one of his tractors with two wood-covered drive wheels, each fifteen feet wide and nine feet in diameter. But his monster wheels weren't the answer to soft earth, and, in 1908, Best sold out to Holt. However, Best's son began making gasoline tractors in 1910, and in 1913 C.L. Best switched to the crawler concept with his "Tracklayer" tractor. The Best Company finally merged with Holt's company, and the resulting Caterpillar Tractor Company emerged as a major manufacturer, continued to make crawlers, and expanded into the fabrication of other kinds of dirt equipment.

Another acquisition of importance in the development of Caterpillar was the purchase of the Russell Road Grader Manufacturing Company of Minneapolis,

South Dakota State Historical Society

169

Koering Concrete Paving Mixer. Portland Cement Association, Skokie, Illinois.

170

one of the country's largest grader makers. This moved Caterpillar into another phase of the road equipment business, and in a substantial way, because Russell was the big name in road machinery in its area of the country.

Allis Chalmers was another user of the moving track system, and one of their products of 1915 is worthy of description. Although it made other, more typical crawlers, Allis sold many of their Tractor-Trucks. Basically a heavy truck with crawler tracks replacing the rear drive wheels, the truck bed included a hoist for dumping the bed-box. Obviously, it was a useful vehicle for hauling over rough terrain, but it also functioned for towing scrapers, rollers or scarifiers.

The Buffalo Steam Roller Company made a large number of its Buffalo-Pitts rollers while Austin-Western Machinery of Chicago and Koehring of Milwaukee were best known for their concrete mixing and handling equipment, but all three companies made various kinds of road equipment. Baker manufactured self-loading four-wheel scrapers; Kilbourne and Jacobs made drag and wheeled scrapers as did (obviously) the Western Wheeled Scraper Company. And so it went.

**Road grader equipped with crawler tracks and capable of very heavy-duty earth work.**

Many companies entered the road machinery business, some for just a short while and others with enduring success. A good bit of machinery came from local blacksmiths and handymen, and they modified and improved some manufactured machinery. New ideas cropped up and became new techniques. These were incorporated into machines, and the machines became more and more efficient, and in turn, made better and better roads.

The development of one major type of equipment still has not been described in this account. It might well be the piece of road making machinery which most people would identify as the most common: the bulldozer. It, too, began as a rather simple and surprisingly ingenious machine. Perhaps the most startling fact about the bulldozer was that it started as a muscle-powered device.

Early contractors frequently faced the challenge of dumping dirt into ravines to fill them for a roadway. Or they needed to push dirt or other fill material into a bog, swamp, or pond as they built a road through the watery area. Getting the dirt over the edge or into the water was a real problem. Road builders could move a pile of earth to the edge of the water or ravine, but how could they push it in? Usually it was done by hand, that is, with men wielding shovels. If some sort of a blade or pushing device could be pushed by a team of mules, that would have done the job nicely. But animals only pulled. Someone finally came up with a way to push earth in front of the team rather than having the team pull the load behind them. One could hook a team to a cart or grader, and as the team pulled, a heavy beam attached to cart or grader, posi-

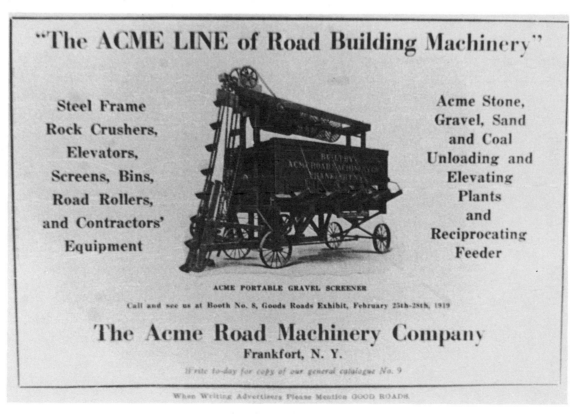

Advertisement for a portable gravel screener manufactured by Acme Road Machinery Company.

tioned between the mules or horses, extended out in front of the team. To the beam was attached a blade, which could then push a load of earth forward.

The Foley Brothers, pioneer railroad builders, were among those who used hand-made bulldozers. Soon steel replaced the wooden beam used originally; steel I-beams were used instead of an oak or hickory beam. Later, the Foleys applied the pushing technique to a steam traction engine. The Western Wheeled Scraper Company, later incorporated into the Austin-Western Company, manufactured the first factory-produced bulldozer, probably in 1914 or 1915. The Russell Manufacturing Company also made a date – pushing machine and called the product a "Bull Dozer" or marsh filler.

Creation of the types of machinery used for highway construction evolved gradually rather than being instant inventions. Holt, Adams, Huber and others were, without question, inventive geniuses. However, the transition which moved some companies from agricultural to construction implements was by no means a quantum leap. The horse-drawn scraper used for smoothing the surface of a farmer's field or excavating a basement could be used in similar fashion to build a road. An agricultural traction engine became an engine for pulling road graders with no modification required. A traction engine was so heavy that it performed the job of road compacting even before some were modified as road rollers. The changeover was natural and nearly spontaneous. Much of the genius involved was the recognition of a new marketplace for existing or slightly modified products.

**Ohio Historical Society's Department of Highways Collection.**

175

A large folder is being distributed by the Buffalo-Pitts Co. of Buffalo, N.Y. It is elaborately illustrated with views of the company's road building machines in operation and with large silhouetted halftones of the machines alone.
-- *Good Roads* magazine for March 1, 1913

We forget that technology is as much structures as it is machines.
-- David P. Billington

No official record of the number of manufacturers [of automobiles] is made, but there are probably seventy-five establishments turning out machines for the trade, while there are many more small concerns which manufacture special machines on order.... There is scarcely a firm that is not behind with orders, and very many state in their advertisements that they cannot accept orders for immediate delivery. New companies are organizing every day....
-- *Outing* magazine for September 1902

# 7
# *Even Model T Fords Contribute*

**J**ust as Galion used a Ford engine to power its roller, many companies used Ford car and truck chassis for a variety of specialized purposes. And, of course, many of these special-purpose vehicles or equipment were of use in road and highway construction. A 1923 article in *Ford Owner and Dealer* reported:

> Designed for the Fordson and the Ford truck is a big line of specialized equipment including concrete mixers, road graders, maintainers, surfacing implements, dump bodies, shovels, loading equipment, drags and numerous other devices built by engineers who have studied the problems of road building, know its requirements and have contributed these things designed to do better work in the great endeavor of highway construction.
>
> Every person engaged in such work owes it to himself as well as to the commonwealth to become acquainted with Ford power to which has been adapted this special equipment....

Of course, not all Model T Fords used in road construction were extensively modified. More than anything else, vehicles used in construction were used for hauling. Runabouts and coupes were stripped of their turtledecks and fitted with a variety of boxes then used for light-duty hauling. Both individuals and companies purchased Model TT one-ton trucks without beds or as bare chassis and then built appropriate attachments for moving an endless variety of materials.

**Big Creek bridge, eastern Wyoming. Coe Library, University of Wyoming.**

Mayo Trail in Pike County, Kentucky. Kentucky Historical Society.

**New Mexico Highway Department.**

Compared to huge modern equipment, Model Ts might appear to be unlikely candidates for road work. However, during the teens and 20s, there was relatively little motorized equipment in use. The major competition for Model Ts were horses and mules. It was the small size, flexibility and low cost of the Fords that enabled construction companies to adopt, and adapt, them. An Indiana contractor who had just finished building six miles of the Lincoln Highway in 1922 described the usefulness of Model T Fords in his project: "They work like a bunch of ants. They fly around here and there, the very spirit of industry." He went on to comment upon the role of horses in construction, indicating that with Ford power units available to the road builder, old Dobbin was obsolete. Comparisons of horses to Fords would indeed "prove odious to the horse."

**Construction supervisors with their Model T roadster pickup. Ohio Historical Society's Ohio Highway Department Collection.**

To demonstrate the value of Ford trucks, a Seattle dealer showed that one Model TT truck equipped with an automatic dump body could haul as much as two full teams of horses. Cost to operate the truck was less than feeding the horses. Clever dealers elsewhere set up pulling contests between Ts and horses, and invariably the horses lost. Road builders soon found that it was both easier and cheaper to handle gasoline in tanks than wagonloads or truckloads of hay and oats.

The Ford Motor Company did not build specialized bodies needed by truck users. Many companies sprang up to build bodies to fit the Model TT chassis

**Loading old brick pavement into a Model TT truck equipped with dump bed. Ohio Historical Society's Ohio Highway Department Collection.**

after the TT was introduced in 1917. The most common bodies used by the road construction industry were "dump trucks." Moving sand, gravel, crushed rock, or earth was more economical by truck than horse-drawn dump wagons. This was especially true when materials had to be moved over considerable distance. So long as relatively flat roads were merely graded and left with an earth surface, horses and mules served well. When gravel, asphalt, or concrete had to be moved long distances, trucks showed a tremendous advantage.

**Model TT Ford one-ton truck ready for service. Ohio Historical Society's Ohio Highway Department Collection.**

Beyond the wide variety of dumping units made for TTs, users equipped regular flatbeds with sideboards and hauled all sorts of material and equipment. TTs moved brick and cut stone to sites where they were laid as pavement and curbs. Tank bodies provided water and oil as needed, both bulk delivery and

Some Ohio Highway Department equipment including both a Model T and a Model TT along with other makes. Ohio Historical Society's Ohio Highway Department Collection.

Ohio Historical Society's Department of Highway Collection.

**This truck was outfitted for delivering batches of concrete. Portland Cement Association, Skokie, Illinois.**

equipped with sprinklers or spreaders. Frequently, Ford trucks functioned as maintenance vehicles by pulling road drags. Grader blades attached to the front of TTs turned the trucks into road machines of sorts and effective snow-plows. Contractors added pumps, powered by the TT engines, to pump water from nearby streams, ponds, or reservoirs into their tank bodies instead of hauling water from greater distances. The pump additions imitated Model T fire trucks, a great quantity of which were in use during the teens and '20s.

One of the most interesting modifications was the "Mixermobile," a seven-cubic-foot cement mixer mounted on a TT chassis. It was equipped with a water tank, a power loader, and a swinging distribution chute. The truck's driveshaft was equipped with a power take-off to turn the mixer. The producer of Mixermobiles, the Milwaukee Concrete Mixer Company, touted the simplicity of installation. "The mixer attachments are so constructed that they can readily be mounted on the Ford truck chassis without the use of any tools other than a wrench and a screwdriver. By releasing four clamps the mixer attachment can be removed and be replaced by a truck body."

Few good ideas had only one taker. The Archer Iron Works of Chicago also produced an early concrete mixer to be mounted on a Ford Model TT chassis.

Using a Ford didn't require a huge increase in the contractor's investment either. In 1917, the bare chassis sold for $600 and by 1924 was down to $370. The price in 1923 for a one-ton TT equipped with a one-and-a-half-yard Winsor Gravity End Dump with enclosed cab, Warford aftermarket transmission, special radius rods, and oversize tires, was $835.66 F.O.B. Detroit. Separate dump bodies, such as the Beard Patented Dump Body, could be purchased. It had trap door dumping between the wheels, could be "installed by anyone in two hours," and was priced at $75. Or the Gar Wood Company marketed a Self Dumper, all steel, for $140. The Anthony Automatic Rocker Dump-

**First road across the Great Smoky Mountains. Pack Memorial Public Library, Asheville, North Carolina.**

ing Body with one-yard capacity was $149.50. The Lawrence Bruder Company of Cincinnati made dump units that varied from the typical style in that they dumped to the side instead of to the back. The Heil Company probably built more different body styles than any other manufacturer. They made at least four dump bodies, a sprinkling tank, a compartment tank, and a concrete batch body for attachment to TT chassis, and many others which were unrelated to the construction business.

Far and away the most unique modification of a TT truck for road work was the "Nail Picker." The nail picker was designed to do just that, pick up nails in the road before they punctured automobile tires. A Model T engine mounted on the bed of a TT truck powered a dynamo which, in turn, produced current for a huge electromagnet suspended behind the truck's rear wheels. The nail picker was produced by the Spring and Forging Company of Roswell, New Mexico. It was first suggested to the company by the New Mexico State High-

The Nailpicker. New Mexico Highway Department.

way Engineer W.C. Davidson, and that highway department purchased several over a period of ten years in the late 20s and early 30s, prior to the paving of many New Mexico highways. Other similar units were built around the country, but apparently Spring and Forging was the only commercial venture in metallic cleansing for roads.

Gravel Road Maintenance- Placing a thin layer of gravel on the road surface.- A view on I C.H.Nº5 north of Circleville, O. Nov. 1918

**Ohio Historical Society's Department of Highways Collection.**

The nail pickers were effective. The *New Mexico Highway Journal* printed "The Tale of a Nail," including this worthy thought:

> Nails accrue on the highways faster than interest on car payments. They fall from trucks, wagons, trailers, and believe it or not, your pleasure car leaves its quota of nails and bits of iron on the highway. Where there is extensive hauling of merchandise, highways receive much more than the usual amount of puncture producing material. This situation cannot be prevented, as the process of distribution is continual, but it can be remedied. The greatest aid to all who operate pneumatic tired vehicles is a machine operated electrically, which rids the highways of this deadly menace.

Purchasers must have agreed as the company boasted a sale as far away as the Ministry of Public Works in Warsaw, Poland, and that "a number of Southern States and Cities are using 'Nail Pickers' as part of their regular highway and street service."

Other firms altered Ford products or major parts thereof for construction work. The C.D. Edwards Manufacturing Company of Albert Lea, Minnesota, merged a Fordson tractor and light road grader to make a motorized, one-man road machine. Mechanically, the tractor was not altered. The grader likewise was changed little but was attached directly to the tractor without a separate hitch. The machine's operator rode the grader in the usual position and operated the tractor with levers connected to the tractor controls with long steel rods. A similar grader pulled by animals required two operators, one to drive the team of horses or mules, the other to operate the grader. Advertising for a

Road construction equipment of Platte County, Wyoming, behind the county courthouse. Wyoming State Archives, Museums and Historical Department.

Model T assigned to the Lake County, Ohio, Engineer's Department. Ohio Historical Society's Ohio Highway Department Collection.

Collins Avenue in Miami Beach during the 1920s. Florida Department of Commerce, Division of Tourism.

somewhat similar machine, the Wehr One-Man Power Grader, described their product as "a combination of the Fordson tractor and a road grader," saying that it was "destined to replace the two units of road work now in ascendancy -- the horse-drawn graders which require two to four men to operate, and the expensive tractor...." This combination was so simple that the conversion was said to require only one hour. The front axle and wheels were to be removed from the tractor, and then it was bolted into the yolk at the rear of the grader. If the contractor needed the tractor for other work, it could be removed from the grader and restored to normal operation just as quickly.

**Maintenance work with a Model TT Ford truck. Ohio Historical Society's Department of Highways Collection.**

At least one modifying manufacturer was successful in converting Fordson tractors into crawler tractors, creating small bulldozers when a blade was attached to the front. A number of other companies tried to find ways to convert the inexpensive Fordson into a crawler that could compete with Caterpillar, CleTrac, and Allis Chalmers, major manufacturers of crawler tractors. The George H. Smith Steel Casting Company of Milwaukee made the Full-Crawler. Anyone could purchase the unit and attach it to a Fordson with no machine work or welding required, not even any holes to drill. Smith advertised that the unit "makes the Fordson tractor the lowest priced, most efficient and most economical light crawler tractor on the market."

Fordsons made an effective base for road rollers, too. One creative contractor devised -- as many surely did although not recorded for history -- an inexpensive roller by bolting an extra pair of wheels to the regular rear wheels. He filled all four wheels with concrete and immediately had a roller. The Austin Western Company built a small road roller around the Fordson, called the "Pup," and had excellent success with it. Galion and Huber, mentioned previously, also used Fordson power plants.

The forerunner of modern front loaders was an accessory made for Fordsons. The Lessman Company of Des Moines built a loader which could lift one-quarter cubic yard and dump it into a truck or wagon. Lessman described it as "really a small steam shovel" that could "fit 95 per cent of all small jobs, allowing one man to do the work of a crew." This device preceded the introduction of hydraulic units and operated by means of cables and winches. Lessman made several models designed to lift different items, but the basic unit of

**Loading earth into a Model TT Ford truck equipped with a dump bed using a Lessman Loader. Ohio Historical Society's Department of Highways Collection.**

**Colorado Highway Historical Society.**

Denver Public Library, Western History Collection.

Model T Ford fording a ford on an Ohio highway detour. Ohio Historical Society's Ohio Highway Department Collection.

all their models could be attached permanently to a tractor in less than one hour.

Another kind of loader could be fitted to the back of a Fordson and was something of a substitute for a New Era Grader. It could load sand, gravel or loose earth and was called the Specialty Fordson Loader. A bucket and conveyor belt operation, it lifted material from the back of the tractor up and over the head of the driver and over the front of the engine, dumping the buckets continuously into a truck or wagon.

The variety of units towed by Fordsons at construction sites, but which could be towed by other tractors as well, was nearly limitless. Other automobile, truck, or tractor companies could have played the same major role in highway construction as Ford played, except that no one else matched the price, size, versatility, or dependability provided by Ford. Indeed, Ford bridged the gap between horse and mule power and the large road equipment that became common in the late 20s. No other manufacturer seemed able to perform this essential function.

Advertisement for one of many units based on the Fordson tractor in *Ford Owner and Dealer.*

I recall to mind particularly one road about a thousand feet across a marsh, a very nice gravel road, and the muskrats would bore into it from the side, and of course the surface crust would break up. I would fill that hole, and then they would dig another hole, and so that work of destruction kept going on continually. And they asked me to make a suggestion about it, and I suggested that they get a small boy with a shot gun...the muskrats got away from the boys.

But in driving over a similar road in the western part of our state, I noticed in an old corduroy road built across a marsh that wherever there was a hollow log there was a muskrat, and he would make that hollow log his home...I took this piece of road that we had been troubled with so much, and every 50 or 100 ft. I would run in a blind drain about 6 or 7 feet at about the surface of the water--a 6 in. pipe, with a T on the end of it. Then I would close up the ends with flat stones, and the muskrats would invariably go in there and they never troubled the road any more after that.

-- *Good Roads*, Feb. 1, 1913

200

# 8

# *Even Tougher Challenges*

**E**arly highway construction, even at its best, was a difficult job, and one without a basic body of information about how things should be done. But in certain parts of the country, the nature of the topography created challenges that tested the ingenuity and, indeed, the courage of road builders. Hills, mountains, rivers, swamps and other wetlands, deserts, sand beaches, sinkhole regions -- these and other features of physiography tried their patience and cre-

**Ferry on the Kentucky River near Boonesborough.**

201

New Battle Mountain Highway on Ocean to Ocean Route. Denver Public Library, Western History Collection.

ativity. In the early years of the century, just the removal of trees and boulders and the solidification of mud and dust were more than adequate challenges.

The most obvious barriers to road construction were mountains. The most common barriers were rivers and streams. But perhaps the most frustrating barriers were those created by fine, shifting sand. Fortunately for America's road builders, there were relatively few such situations.

Perhaps the best known of the sand barriers was the Algodones Dunes in southeastern California. Most other major dunes in the United States could be built around rather than through, the White Sands of New Mexico or the Great Sand Dunes of Colorado being notable examples. But the Algodones lay across the direct route from Yuma, Arizona, to San Diego, California. To skirt these dunes to the north would require building some forty miles northwest and then thirty miles south again. To go around them to the south would require the road to cross the border into Mexico.

Three unusual roads were built across the dunes prior to the eventual, traditional road paved with asphaltic concrete. The first attempt was a road made of a mat of brush. A few heavy cars passing over the brush ground it to bits.

**Denver Public Library, Western History Collection.**

Cars trying to follow this primitive attempt at road making ended up in the dunes, on a "road" no better than soft sand, and probably stuck.

Next came the wooden plank road of 1915, financed primarily by public subscription and constructed partly by volunteers from the area. The road consisted of two-inch by twelve-inch planks. One pair of planks was laid side by side for the wheels of one side of the car, and another pair of planks was laid for the other wheels; a ribbon of sand showed between them. The plank tracks were tied together with cross ties, much like a railroad.

The city of San Diego furnished the lumber for the road. The dunes were located just east of the agriculturally rich Impe-

**Plank road across Arizona dunes. From the collections of Henry Ford Museum and Greenfield Village.**

rial Valley, and valley towns supplied the workers: "Finally after six months of discouraging work, the first plank road was completed."

There were two major problems in traveling this type road. One was excess traffic. It was strictly a one-lane road, and when a driver encountered another car, one of the cars had to back up to special turnouts prepared for such situations. Many times the drivers decided to pass with each one having the interior pair of wheels on the wooden track and the other on sand. This attempt was often a disaster. Persons traveling in a Model T Ford might be able to lift their car back on to the road. For heavy cars, a tow was essential. Nevertheless, the road was a success for many cars traveling across it. However, the

second problem actually stopped travel. During the spring of the year when high winds blew, dunes shifted, covering the road. Often the sand drifts had to be shoveled away. The road lasted a year, the sand under rolling car tires grinding away the wood.

Then in 1916 the California Highway Commission constructed an improved plank road. This time the planks were laid at right angles to the path of the road. Materials arrived by railroad, and twelve-foot sections were constructed next to the railroad, then hauled to the road site by ten-horse teams. Extra sections of planking, eight feet wide and placed every half mile (another account placed the turnouts a bit further apart at every 1000 yards), allowed for vehicles to pass one another on the one-lane road. Again, there was the problem of shifting sand dunes. The state of California spent some $35,000 annually to keep the road passable, clearing the sand with teams and scrapers. The plank road, seven-and-one-half miles long, lasted just a year. Then it was replanked in 1917, and again and again. The dunes were not crossed by pavement until 1926.

Of course, the pounding of vehicles gradually deteriorated the planks. Drivers recalled the roughness by suggesting that, at the speed of twelve miles per hour, one "would see double." At twenty miles per hour, "the front wheels shimmied so bad a car was in danger of bouncing off the planks."

205

**Arizona plank road: A detour was caused by shifting dunes. From the collections of Henry Ford Museum and Greenfield Village.**

206

**Arizona plank road: a turnout for cars meeting one another on the single lane road. From the collections of Henry Ford Museum and Greenfield Village.**

The single-lane construction played a role in one of California's most spectacular traffic jams. Yes, a traffic jam occurred as early as 1925. A movie company was filming in the area, and many sightseers arrived at the plank road to view the stars. It was not long before the traffic was bumper to bumper for miles, and there was no way to move. According to one of those trapped in the dunes, "In order to clear the road, several men would get hold of the lighter cars, turn them around and head them back toward Yuma, but it was 2 and 1/2 days before the tangle was all straightened out and I could go on my way."

Another desert highway of unusual construction was completed in 1925 in Utah, crossing the mud flats and salt beds of the Great Salt Lake Desert. The new road was greatly desired because it reduced tremendously the travel distance between Salt Lake City and Wendover, on the Utah-Nevada border, for motorists headed for San Francisco and the California coast. To build the road on a bed of salt, which could be dissolved by water, was a challenge indeed. However, the salt beds remained stable in the heavy salt brine characteristic of the region through most of the year. Only fresh water dissolved the road bed. Tons and tons of clay were brought to the road and dumped to protect the road bed from fresh water, much as levees are used along rivers to protect farm land from overflow. Construction required sixteen months with many miles of the road bed submerged in brine.

From Anderson's *Modern Road Building and Maintenance* published by the Hercules Powder Company.

An altogether novel technique for road building emerged and then disappeared in the arid Southwest. Wind that was a problem in the California dunes became a positive factor in this situation. The desert wind was the driving force behind this method. Ignoring conventional techniques, the district highway superin-

From Anderson's *Modern Road Building and Maintenance* published by the Hercules Powder Company.

**Boone Tunnel adjacent to Brooklyn Bridge, Jessamine County, Kentucky. Kentucky Historical Society.**

tendent for east central New Mexico built eighty miles of road across sand wastes by making a trench down to the solid clay beneath the sand and letting the desert wind do the rest. After clearing the right of way of grass and weeds, the sand was removed from a strip twelve feet wide with Fresno scrapers. Wind widened the strip from twelve feet to thirty-five feet or more. A little grading to smooth the clay surface then provided a good road.

The great arid lands of the West challenged drivers of motor cars just as they had drivers of horse or oxen teams who preceded them. Both heat and quantities of dust exceeded what was found in other parts of the country. In addition, there was the paucity of roads caused by the sparse population and both mountain ranges and rough country between the ranges. A 1913 issue of *Ford Times* described the trip of noted magazine writer Helen Lukens Gaut from Pasadena, California, to Coachella, Arizona.

> The trip is a most arduous one for anyone to undertake and would never have been attempted by a woman less intrepid. The road she traversed is one of the roughest and worst in the world. In most places it is no road at all, but simply a trail leading

**Mrs. Hellen Gaut at the wheel of the Ford runabout which she drove alone from Pasadena to Coachella, Arizona, and back.**

**Auto precedes horse across this bridge. Colorado Historical Society.**

across a country abounding in ruts and hummocks and strewn with bolders [sic]. In other places the sand, of a fine shifting variety, allows the car to sink almost axle deep.

The car she drove was a 1911 Model T Ford torpedo runabout.

The challenges to road builders in the West went beyond the matter of sand deserts. As noted before, the most obvious barriers were mountains. In the desert Southwest states of Arizona and New Mexico, it was possible for main highways to be built around mountain ranges. But from northern New Mexico through Colorado and Wyoming to Montana and Idaho, the Rocky Mountains were continuous. There was no way to go around, leaving builders with no choice but to search for the lowest and most accessible passes through the mountains. As was true throughout the country, the path of new roads constructed for automobiles followed wagon roads which, in turn, followed horse trails. When early road builders sought to cross a mountain range with their road, they chose known routes. They entered the mountains by following

**National Automotive History Collection, Detroit Public Library.**

streams up valleys and canyons, and headed for the easiest passes to cross. Then they followed ridges until valleys or canyons on the other side provided egress from the mountains. Construction was extremely difficult and often very dangerous for the workers.

A project in northern New Mexico, described by Kenneth Balcomb in his *The Red River Hill*, was typical of the struggles during construction of mountain roads. The first job to be done was to remove the trees from the future road bed. To knock down firs and pines, a carefully placed charge of dynamite under the roots was effective. Aspens were rather unstable because of a weak root system, and these could be pulled down by a hefty team. A worker climbed a tree and attached a heavy rope some ten or fifteen feet up. The rope was hitched to a team of horses or mules, and, pulling to one side and then the other, the tree would come crashing down.

Boulders in the road could be more difficult to remove than the trees. Men lifted rocks as large as they could carry and put them into horse-drawn carts called, appropriately enough, "stone boats." Larger boulders were broken up using dynamite with a technique called the "adobe" method. The dynamite was placed against a flat surface and held in place by mud. When the dynamite exploded, it cracked the rock into smaller pieces.

The most difficult and hazardous aspect of the construction resulted from steepness of the slopes and instability of the bare slopes. "It was impossible to get teams and equipment on some stretches until a shelf at least four feet wide had been dug by hand." Then a team could operate side by side although without much maneuvering room.

Principal equipment used on the job, other than picks and shovels, included large beam plows used to loosen earth, and slip scrapers and fresno scrapers to move earth from one place to another. The fresno operator hung the reins of his two-, three- or four-horse team around his neck. Then with a piece of rope attached to the control bar, which extended back from the body of the scraper, the operator tipped the fresno forward so that it would scoop into the loosened dirt. Then he leveled the fresno with the bar, and the team pulled it to the edge. The operator then lifted up the bar, tilting the fresno forward and dumping the contents over the edge. That was a critical moment as the operator had to hold tightly to the rope to prevent the scraper from toppling over the edge after its load. Tight quarters made every minute exciting, to say the least.

> The fresno operator worked under the most difficult conditions. He had to contend with the vagaries of a team...who, hour in and hour out during the day, might get nervous and plunge or balk. Loading the material ranging from fine dust to sizeable rocks

Columbia River Scenic Highway constructed 1914-1922, Hood River County, Oregon. Oregon Department of Transportation.

was very difficult and not always successful, and the most trying of all were the dangers encountered in dumping the load over the embankment. Anything might happen. These operations were carried on in a pall of dust with both team and driver being harassed by horseflies and the pestiferous grey [sic] hackles.... Many times the fresno would get away over the bank, threatening to pull the team over too, only to be recovered by all hands assisting the team in pulling it up. Three times that season, however, a team was pulled down the slope and each was a terrible experience, although only one time was it fatal to horses.

Teams of mules were much gentler in temperament and when, in two instances, mule teams went over the edge, they struggled mightily as they fell and rolled. But when they came to a stop thirty or so feet down the slope, they simply lay until rescued by cutting away harnesses and leading back to the "road." When horse teams went over the edge with their fresnos, they died of fright or were crippled so badly that they had to be shot.

For much mountain road building, men, mules, horses, and equipment were not as important as dynamite. Indeed, routes which passed through canyons literally were blasted from the rock walls of the canyons. Among the important reference books found in the offices of most civil engineers and road contractors of the time was a manual produced by the Hercules Powder Company. As was true for mining and railroad construction through mountains, the expert in placing and firing dynamite charges was a most important person in road construction.

Among many quality roads constructed in scenic locations, the Columbia River Highway in Oregon stands out. Initially surveyed in 1913, partially opened for traffic in 1915, and brought to its completion over the full length in 1922, this road set the standards for mountain highway construction for decades to follow. It is important to note that, some eighty years after the beginning of the project, the Old Columbia River Highway is included in the National Register of Historic Places. An original highway of significant length, with its bridges, tunnels and magnificent scenery, creates one of the most unusual historic districts on the Register and certainly one of the longest and narrowest.

**1918 Model T on an Oregon mountain highway with Mount Hood in the background. Bill White collection.**

One of the documents recommending conservation and reuse of the abandoned highway said, in 1981, it "was so carefully integrated with the landscape that it became a work of art in itself." The engineer who surveyed the gorge and laid out the road was struck with its beauty and the opportunity presented, saying, "Instinctively there came a prayer for strong men and that we might have sense enough to do the thing in the right way...so as not to mar what God had put there."

The survey crew spent weeks climbing and hiking through the gorge to locate the most beautiful sights and then determine how the proposed road could reach them, yet not mar the cliffs and wooded terrain. Their success was demonstrated by praise from General George W. Goethals, builder of the Panama Canal: "Splendid engineering" and "absolutely without equal in America for scenic interest." President Theodore Roosevelt pronounced: "You have

Shepherd's Dell Arch Bridge built in 1914, Columbia River Scenic Highway. Oregon Department of Transportation.

in the Columbia Highway the most remarkable engineering in the United States, which for scenic grandeur is not equaled anywhere."

Not only was the road one which protected the scenic grandeur of the region through which it passed, the road itself contributed to the scenery. Most of the bridges were attractive concrete arches, relatively uncommon for the time. In sections where it was judged to be overly difficult to cut the roadway into the side of a cliff, half viaducts were constructed. Here the half of the road next to the river was a continuous bridge while the half next to the cliff was in space originally occupied by rock that had been blasted away. Other sections of the road were built partly or entirely over a roadbed supported with dry masonry.

Dynamite also was important in the construction of a very different type of highway. In this case it was a matter of crossing the Florida Everglades, and the barrier to conquer was shallow water rather than mountains.

**Completed roadbed for Tamiami Trail across the Florida Everglades. Florida State Archives.**

Digging a canal beside the roadbed for Tamiami Trail across the Florida Everglades. Florida State Archives.

In 1915, the state of Florida had excellent railroads. But the southern portion of the peninsula only had automobile roads adjacent to the two coasts. Along the west coast there was no hard-surfaced road south of Venice. And according to Florida road contractor L.B. McLeod, "Actually a hard top road back in the early 1920s was anything that your car didn't mire down in." Usually the surface was rock or slag from the Birmingham steel mills.

A cross-state highway would be especially important for citizens who lived in Fort Myers and along the gulf coast to the south. They were effectively isolated from the rest of the state when it came to automobile travel. On the east coast, Miami businessmen were anxious to extend their markets. In-between was a 100-mile wasteland with no population. The wasteland extended nearly 100 miles from north to south as well. Islands along the western coast were

**Shovel at work during construction of Tamiami Trail across the Florida Everglades. Florida State Archives.**

222

**Rock for roadbed of Tamiami Trail, blasted and dug from Everglades floor, creating canal at left. Florida State Archives.**

retreats for moonshiners and bootleggers, and law and order were practically nonexistent. A newspaper of the area described the southern end of the Florida peninsula as "The Last Remaining Frontier." The region certainly was at odds with our images of a vacation wonderland. As is always the case in building a new highway, the first step was scouting a feasible route. Seminole Indians from the area led surveyors who traveled across the Everglades in canoes. The dangerous trip through muck and water revealed that the greatest depth of water encountered was no more than six feet, a depth where construction might be possible. With this information, promoters gained the necessary support in the state capital and then convinced the voters of Dade County (where Miami is county seat and which is a huge county, stretching west from Miami two-thirds of the way across the state) to pass a bond issue with a quarter of a million dollars directed toward construction of the road. As part of the process of convincing people that a road across the Everglades was really possible, its

Dredging during construction of the Tamiami Trail across the Florida Everglades. Florida State Archives.

Candler's bridge near Corbin, Kentucky, circa 1900. Kentucky Historical Society.

Construction of the Galveston causeway, 1909-1912. Courtesy of the Rosenberg Library, Galveston, Texas.

major supporter, Captain J.F. Jaudon of Miami, walked across the Everglades...twice.

The roadway was referred to by a number of names, including "Miami to Marco Highway" from the terminal cities (the latter actually only a hamlet), and the "Atlantic to Gulf Boulevard." Because the road would connect the state's major eastern and western cities, Miami and Tampa, combining the two names provided the "Tamiami Trail," and that name stuck.

At first the builders attempted to create a roadbed by spreading a layer of crushed rock over the underlying limestone. However, they just could not haul in enough rock to keep the road above water and muck during the rainy part of the year. During the dry season, some of the muck dried out to the point of resembling peat, and it would catch fire and burn. They decided then to use the material at hand -- the limestone that lay beneath the Everglade swamps. Using dynamite, a canal was blasted and dug for ninety miles; the limestone taken from the canal became a roadbed beside it. To say that they dug a canal doesn't do justice to the difficulty of the task. Drilling equipment sank from sight into the mud and muck. Horses and mules, likewise, bogged down and had to be dug and pulled out, sometimes requiring hours to extricate a single team.

During the peak of construction, contractors exploded more than 40,000 pounds of dynamite per mile of road. After the dynamiting, they moved dredges into place. At its best, progress moved as rapidly as two miles in a month. In total, though, it was a slow process, finally completed in 1928.

When discouragement reached its peak in 1923, an important step in the political process for the

Traffic on the newly completed Galveston causeway, circa 1912. Courtesy of the Rosenberg Library, Galveston, Texas.

The old and the new in bridges and highways, early 1920s. North Carolina Division of Archives and History.

Tamiami Trail was a motorcade across the swamps, following the approximate route of the future highway. Ten cars started the trek, leaving from Fort Myers. Nine of the cars were Model T Fords, seven of which made it to Miami. One large, powerful car began the trip but ended up abandoned after a short way. When the naysayers, surprised that automobiles had actually crossed the Everglades, quieted down, public opinion fired up, and the project was underway again.

Water was a problem wherever roads were built, just as it had been in Florida. The technology for building bridges suitable for automobile roads was ready and waiting because of the experience of bridge building for railroads. It was merely a matter of placing bridges along roadways rather than railways. Many of the one-lane bridges used for highways were exact duplicates of railroad bridges. (For a simply written but thorough treatment of different variet-

**Toll bridge in Nicholas County, Kentucky, photographed in 1910. Roy L. Shannon Collection.**

ies of bridges and the way they were constructed, see Chapter 3 of David Weitzman's *Traces of the Past, A Field Guide To Industrial Archaeology*.)

As time went on, new types of bridges and culverts came into use. In arid New Mexico, the State Highway Department employed an inexpensive yet important method for their highways to cross intermittent streams of which there were a great many in that state. For decades before, wagons and then automobiles had forded shallow streams, many of which, in the Southwest, ran only periodically. The highway department simply paved stream crossings or arroyo crossings with concrete. The road was passable unless water became unusually deep. They simply gave fords a more formal treatment.

Gradually, bridges replaced that more dramatic method for crossing major streams, the ferry. Ferries were commonplace in the early 1900s: some large vessels, some small, some simply actuated by the stream's current while some were driven by massive steam engines. The vast majority were privately owned

**Bridge construction workers and half a bridge. Tennessee State Archives.**

but a few were owned by cities or counties and a few by states.

From cast iron or wooden culverts to the Brooklyn Bridge, transportation contractors of the late 19th century handled their water barriers successfully. Bridge designers moved from wood to cast iron, wrought iron, steel and then poured concrete. During the 1930s and thereafter, Wyoming highway engineers, in their dry climate, moved back to using wood again for many of their bridges. Regardless of materials from which a bridge was built, bridge evolution was a matter of changing structure to accommodate more and faster vehicles. Of course, this evolution is the same as that of the on-ground part of the highway.

**Shaker ferry on the Kentucky River, Mercer County, Kentucky.**

**A ferry and Fort Boonesborough Memorial Bridge. Kentucky Historical Society.**

**Topeka Bridge and Iron Company constructing an Arizona bridge. Kansas State Historical Society.**

**Major bridge building project in 1920. North Carolina Division of Archives and History.**

**Poured concrete bridge construction, 1917, from front. Ohio Historical Society's Department of Highways Collection.**

**Bridge work. Kansas State Historical Society.**

Poured concrete bridge construction, 1917, from side. Ohio Historical Society's Department of Highways Collection.

Replacement of a steel truss bridge with a concrete bridge on left. North Carolina Division of Archives and History.

New Mexico Highway Department

237

**Ohio River bridge under construction near Paducah, Kentucky. Kentucky Historical Society.**

Boarding a ferry in 1907. National Automotive History Collection, Detroit Public Library.

239

**Mississippi River ferry at Cassville, Wisconsin.**

**Roy L. Shannon Collection.**

241

**Billboard or bridge? Ohio Historical Society.**

**From Diel's Missouri Highways.**

Rolling lift bridge in Elizabeth City, North Carolina, in 1922. North Carolina Division of Archives and History.

Floating bridge, Summit County, Ohio. Ohio Historical Society.

Stone arch bridge and patriotically dressed motorists. Ohio Historical Society.

**Suspension bridge. Colorado Historical Society.**

Unusual cable-bridge over the Gila River in southwestern New Mexico, circa 1915. Harlan Collection, Western New Mexico University.

A car ready to cross the cable-bridge over the Gila River in southwestern New Mexico. Harlan Collection, Western New Mexico University.

S-shape bridge on old National Road near Hendrysburg, Ohio, with new highway at left (soon to be given U.S. 40 designation). National Archives print, Ohio Historical Society.

**S-shape bridge on National Road near Cambridge, Ohio. Photographed in 1933. Ohio Historical Society.**

# 9
# *How Do You Get There?*

**E**arly automobile tourists faced tough challenges whenever they drove their Duryeas, Reos, Buicks, Oldsmobiles, Wintons, or Schachts beyond the city limits of their home towns. As if it wasn't enough that the roads and highways between cities and towns were nearly impassable, finding one's way to the next town along those roads and highways was extremely difficult. In the early

**Library of Congress.**

1900s, there were few road maps or road atlases such as we use today. A few guide books were available, but these focused on main routes. Drivers could select only a few places to go in order for the guides to help.

The primary method for finding one's way was to stop and ask, and such stops came frequently. Many, if not most, of the farmers who could be asked for directions between towns didn't know much about roads, even a few miles from their farms. Unless on the route to the county seat or other nearby community, farmers didn't know how to go. The roads in the next county were a total mystery to most folks in 1905.

Of course, there always was the possibility of trial and error and this actually was an important technique for early automobilists. A driver simply headed in the right direction, selecting the most worn path whenever more than one choice of roads was available. Drivers gathered information on their Sunday afternoon excursions and shared the information with other automobile drivers until the "road lore" of an area was known. Many drivers recorded the information in their own log books for later use, creating the first, although informal, road guides.

A camaraderie developed among early motorists, and, when a community could boast a sufficient number of automobiles, it resulted in the formation of a club or society. Road lore, which first passed orally from motorist to motorist at club meetings, and then became handwritten notes, formed the basis for guidebooks published by automobile clubs. Sketches produced by drivers became crude maps. When polished up a bit, these sketched maps found their way, too, into guidebooks.

Local clubs sprang up all over the country. Clubs in some of the larger cities joined with similar groups in founding the American Automobile Association in 1902. As early as

**Home-built camping trailer, circa 1930.**

**Stuck in the mud in the middle of July on an Ohio highway. Ohio Historical Society.**

1905, the AAA became involved in helping members find their way, publishing a small road map of Staten Island, New York. Of course, the auto club members were interested in touring and maps or guidebooks for their tours, but they also wanted new roads and improvements in existing roads (see pages 32-34 and 46) -- and for good reason.

Automobilists had a few maps available to them which could provide guidance about how to get to the next city. These were prepared by a different category of tourist -- those who traveled by bicycle. The League of American Wheelmen and other bicycle clubs encouraged cyclists to take their cycles to the open road. Included in their activities were group tours and, of course, production of guides and maps with information that would allow cyclists, in groups or as individuals, to ride between cities. However, the maps produced by the wheelmen were of limited value to automobile drivers because some of the marked routes, though adequate for bicycles, were not wide enough for cars.

Another kind of map was readily available in the 1890s and the first two decades of the 20th century -- railroad maps. These were not directly useful in terms of the routes autos could travel, but railroad maps offered two potential contributions to touring automobilists. One was providing a base map upon

253

which the automobilist could draw representations of routes for automobiles discovered while touring. Actually, many of the oldest road maps were simply railroad maps to which the publisher added the chief roads with colored lines. The other use was for locations of railroad bridges across streams. Some roads used by automobilists crossed streams without using bridges; the automobiles simply forded the streams. At times of high water, the automobiles either could not cross the stream or found an alternative way to cross, namely, using a railroad bridge.

Until 1915, the majority of travelers piloted their horseless carriages following the directions contained in guidebooks and, indeed, various guidebooks

**First automobile in Clarksville, Tennessee, in 1902, en route from Toledo, Ohio, to Hot Springs, Arkansas.**

remained popular for many years thereafter. The country's most prominent map historian, Walter W. Ristow of the Library of Congress, described guidebooks:

The first Official Automobile Blue Book, covering eastern United States, was published in 1901. It proved to be an essential source of information for American motorists, and established a standard for automobile guidebooks. Four carefully prepared maps were issued as supplements to the 1901 Blue Book. During the first decade or so of the new century, roadbooks were the preferred motoring guides.... The promotional value of road guides was early recognized, and some of the best ones were distributed by automobile and tire companies.

CYCLISTS
# ROAD MAP
OF THE
# HUDSON RIVER
DISTRICT,
## NEW YORK.

Around Copley Square.

Published by
**Geo. H. Walker & Co.**
Harcourt Street, Boston, Mass.
One Block from Huntington Avenue Station.

**Cyclists' road map printed by Walker and Company of Boston, copyright 1897.**

The Hartford Rubber Company issued, in 1905, a small route book, titled *Automobile Good Roads and Tours*. The guide, which sold for two dollars, described tours in the New York City vicinity. It included a page-size map and a running description and log of the route. A decade later, the B.F. Goodrich Company introduced its *Goodrich Route Books*, which were distributed free to motorists. Some twenty different books were prepared in the years 1912 to 1917.... The White Motor Company of Cleveland claimed that its *White Route Book*, published in 1907 and 1908,

Goodrich.
pix p. 287-289 →

# HOW TO USE THE BLUE BOOK

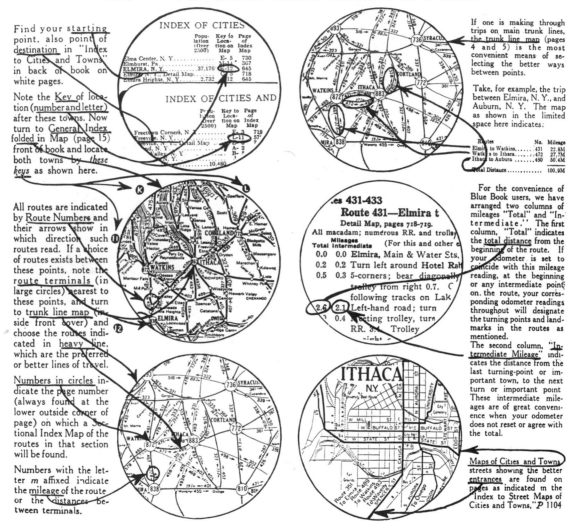

Find your starting point, also point of destination in "Index to Cities and Towns" in back of book on white pages.

Note the Key of location (number and letter) after these towns. Now turn to General Index folded in Map (page 15) front of book and locate both towns by these keys as shown here.

All routes are indicated by Route Numbers and their arrows show in which direction such routes read. If a choice of routes exists between these points, note the route terminals (in large circles) nearest to these points, and turn to trunk line map (inside front cover) and choose the routes indicated in heavy line, which are the preferred or better lines of travel.

Numbers in circles indicate the page number (always found at the lower outside corner of page) on which a Sectional Index Map of the routes in that section will be found.

Numbers with the letter m affixed indicate the mileage of the route or the distances between terminals.

INDEX OF CITIES

| | Popu- lation (Over 2500) | Key to Loca- tion on Index Map | Page of Index Map |
|---|---|---|---|
| Elma Center, N. Y. | | E- 5 | 730 |
| Elmhurst, Pa. | | 3 | 367 |
| ELMIRA, N. Y. | 37,176 | A-12 | 645 |
| Elmira, N. Y., Detail Map. | | 3 | 718 |
| Elmira Heights, N. Y. | 2,732 | 12 | 645 |

INDEX OF CITIES AND

| | Popu- lation (Over 2500) | Key to Loca- tion on Index Map | Page of Index Map |
|---|---|---|---|
| Freetown Corners, N. | | E- 3 | 719 |
| Freeville, N. Y. | | | 57 |
| ..., N. Y., Detail Map | | | 57 |
| ..., N. Y. | | A- 2 | |
| Valley ... N. Y. | | B- 1 | |
| ... | 10,480 | | |

If one is making through trips on main trunk lines, the trunk line map (pages 4 and 5) is the most convenient means of selecting the better ways between points.

Take, for example, the trip between Elmira, N. Y., and Auburn, N. Y. The map as shown in the limited space here indicates:

| Routes | No. | Mileage |
|---|---|---|
| Elmira to Watkins | 431 | 22.8M |
| Watkins to Ithaca | 472 | 27.7M |
| Ithaca to Auburn | 480 | 50.4M |
| Total Distance | | 100.9M |

For the convenience of Blue Book users, we have arranged two columns of mileages "Total" and "Intermediate." The first column, "Total" indicates the total distance from the beginning of the route. If your odometer is set to coincide with this mileage reading, at the beginning or any intermediate point on the route, your corresponding odometer readings throughout will designate the turning points and landmarks in the routes as mentioned.

The second column, "Intermediate Mileage" indicates the distance from the last turning-point or important town, to the next turn or important point These intermediate mileages are of great convenience when your odometer does not reset or agree with the total.

Maps of Cities and Towns streets showing the better entrances are found on pages as indicated in the Index to Street Maps of Cities and Towns," P 1104

## Route 431—Elmira t

Detail Map, pages 718-719.

All macadam; numerous RR. and trolley

Mileages

| Total | Intermediate | |
|---|---|---|
| 0.0 | 0.0 | Elmira, Main & Water Sts. |
| 0.2 | 0.2 | Turn left around Hotel Ra... |
| 0.5 | 0.3 | 5-corners; bear diagonally trolley from right 0.7. C... following tracks on Lak... |
| 2.6 | 2.1 | Left-hand road; turn |
| | 0.4 | ...eeting trolley, turn RR. 3.... Trolley |

The above illustrations are examples only and the route numbers and mileages may not correspond to the present data in this year's volume.

**The instruction pages from the *Official Automotive Blue Book* for 1916, the "Standard Road Guide of America," telling users how to follow routes.**

The RICHMOND

American and European Fire-proof

TIMOTHY MURPHY Prop.

Little Falls N.Y.

SYRACUSE
75 MI. FROM SYRACUSE
225 MI. FROM BUFFALO

75 MI. FROM ALBANY
225 MI. FROM NEW YORK
ALBANY

100 Rooms
50 Rooms with Bath;

A hotel you will visit on every succeeding trip through the scenic Valley of the Mohawk

*In the Heart of the Mohawk Valley*

dangerous trolley crossings beyond; rejoin trolley from right 20.0.

22.1  6.8  Fork, keep left with one line of trolley on W. Main St.

22.4  0.3  **Little Falls**; Main & Ann Sts.

    The Richmond, Main & Ann Sts.
    Ross' Garage, 44 W. Main St.
    Union Garage, Lansing St.

Straight thru with trolley, which ends 22.7  Continue downgrade under RRs. 22.9—23.0, curving left past old suspension bridge.

    From this point can be seen, across the river, the home of and monument to Gen. Nicholas Herkimer, the former taken over and repaired by the State in 1915. From this homestead, Gen. Herkimer marched his Dutch farmers to the relief of Fort Stanwix in 1777, resulting in the battle of Oriskany, one of the turning points in the Revolution. To reach it, turn right across suspension bridge and then left on poor road along canal.

Cross concrete bridge over East Canada Creek 29.4, coming into Main St.

32.7  10.3  **St. Johnsville.**  P. O. on left.

Straight thru on Main St.  Avoid left fork 34.1.

    This left fork is short-cut to Johnstown and Gloversville—good in dry weather.
    On the right 36.0 is the old Palatine Church, erected by the settlers from the Palatinate in 1770, and used both for worship and as a refuge from Indians. It is one of the principal landmarks of the Mohawk Valley and well preserved; services every Sunday.

38.6  5.9  **Nelliston.**  Straight thru on main road.

    Right-hand road across bridge leads to **Fort Plain.**

41.5  2.9  **Palatine Bridge.**  Straight thru on main road.

    Right-hand road is **Route 294** to Cooperstown.
    Fort Van Alstine (or Fort Rensselaer), Canajoharie, now a club and museum, is well worth a visit.

Follow main road along valley—fine views to the south. Cross RR. at **Yost's Sta.** on right 47.8.  Cross RR. and iron bridge 52.8.  Join trolley from left 52.9 and follow same into

53.1  11.6  **Fonda.**  Station on right.

    Brunswick Hotel, on left.
    Left-hand road is **Route 315** to Johnstown, Gloversville and Northville.
    Just beyond center of Fonda, pass right-hand road crossing bridge to Fultonville, where left turn leads to Auriesville, place of martyrdom of Father Joques, 1641, and location of famous shrine.

Straight ahead on macadam along river and RR.  Ascend Tribes Hill, dangerous trolley crossing part-way up 58.3.

                  **Page 731**

**Facing pages from the *Official Automobile Blue Book* for 1916, which show route (or trip) 293. This volume includes over 600 trips in New York and Canada in 1,132 pages.**

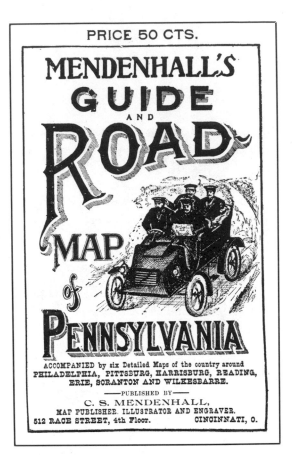

Cover of a 1905 road map and guide.

One of the road maps distributed by the B.F. Goodrich Rubber Company. This one, copyrighted in 1920, includes a list of some 106 branches of The Goodrich Travel and Transport Bureau.

had a circulation of "more than twice that of any other publication containing road directions."

Perhaps the most interesting of the guidebooks were those which included numerous photographs and based their directions upon those photos. *Photographic Automobile Maps* produced by the H. Sargent Michaels Company were the most common. The major turns in the routes were marked by arrows superimposed upon the photos. Although the books were not accurately named in terms of current usage for the word "map," they were certainly useful additions to the driving kit of the early motorist. Apparently the first of the Michaels books came out in 1905.

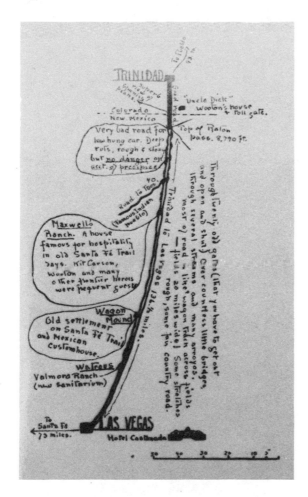

**Hand-drawn map from Emily Post's book, *By Motor to the Golden Gate*, 1916.**

In 1907, G.S. Chapin copyrighted a similar type of product under the name of *Photo-Auto Maps*, which guided tourists between major midwestern cities. These guides claimed that their "descriptive matter calls attention to every point of interest and attraction...enabling him to enjoy all the pleasures to be had on such an excursion." Later, Rand McNally and Company took over publication and marketing of the *Photo-Auto Maps*. As bad as the roads were, a considerable number of intrepid tourists set out to see the country, some on trips of great distance. Among the rich and famous who did so were Emily Post and her son, E.M. Post. Ms. Post published a book describing their 1915 travels, titled *By Motor To The Golden Gate* (Appleton, 1916). Included with the accounts of driving difficulties, adventures, and some deluxe dinners in posh hotels, were many hand-drawn maps of their route. The maps were of sufficient quality that

Cover of a 1912 strip map of a highway across Iowa, claimed to be the "Iowa Official Transcontinental Route."

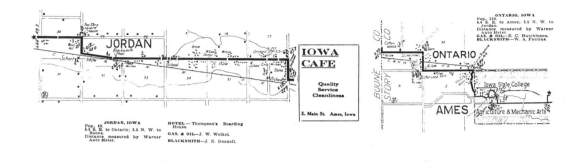

**Adjoining pages of the "Iowa Official Transcontinental Route" with maps showing small parts of the route.**

# GENERAL MAP
## IOWA OFFICIAL TRANS-CONTINENTAL ROUTE

## LEGEND

| | | | |
|---|---|---|---|
| HOUSE | ■ | WOODEN BRIDGE | ■ ■ |
| SCHOOL | ▲ | STEEL BRIDGE | ■ ■ |
| CHURCH | ✝ | CONCRETE BRIDGE | ■ ■ |
| WINDMILL | ■ | CULVERT | ■ ■ |
| TROLLEY | ▬▬▬ | CEMETERY | t |
| RAILROAD | ▬▬ | TREE | |
| MAILBOX (Figures denote Number of Boxes) 42 | | SIGN | |

**Overall strip map of "Iowa Official Transcontinental Route."**

261

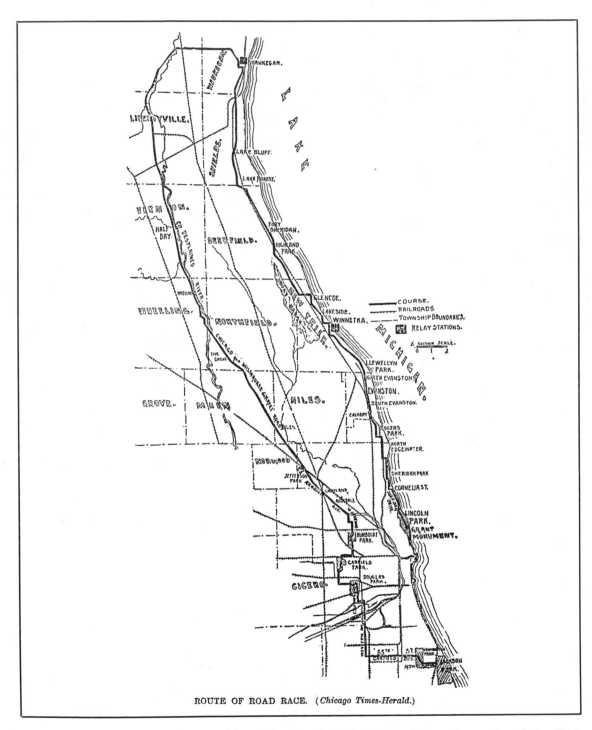

ROUTE OF ROAD RACE. (*Chicago Times-Herald.*)

**The first automobile road map printed in the United States shows the route of the first automobile race, sponsored by the *Chicago Times-Herald*, on Nov. 2, 1895. From volume 1, number 1 of *The Horseless Age* magazine.**

they could be followed across the country.

The road map as we know it today, showing all of the roads in some area (such as a county, state, or group of states) did not arrive on the scene until 1914. Maps prior to that time were strip maps, that is, maps which illustrated a single route. Typically, there would be a strip map of the route, enlarged sections of the route, and advertisements purchased by merchants along the route. These ads provided important information to the tourists, such as where to stop for the night, obtain repairs, or buy gasoline. Because most people in the early teens continued to do most of their "important" traveling by railroad, the majority of trips by automobile were pleasure trips. Therefore, the strip maps included information about local points of interest, scenery, and possible side trips, often with pictures of points of special interest.

The very first automobile road map printed in the United States probably was a map printed in the Chicago Times-Herald of the route for the first U.S. automobile race. That race, some fifty-four miles long, was intended to demonstrate the practicality of travel by self-propelled vehicles and included a $5000

**Denver Public Library, Western History Collection.**

**Texaco dealer, Burlington, Vermont. McAllister Collection, Special Collections, University of Vermont Library.**

prize for the winning car, that of J. Frank Duryea. The course ran from Jackson Park in Chicago to Waukegan, Illinois and back to Lincoln Park in Chicago. Duryea followed the race route by using the map torn out of the newspaper.

There were a number of reasons why the road map, which folded up to pocket size, did not develop sooner, even though it certainly was a handy device. First, the demand was small. Millions of people traveled in 1900, riding the railroads, but just a few thousand drove cars. By 1910, the number of motor cars licensed in the United States still was less than a million. And many of the owners, knowing the nature of the existing highways, were not so bold as to venture out into the country on any extended trip.

Second, it was difficult to determine just what should be included on the maps, owing to the fact that there were no national or state highways. Throughout most of the nation, there weren't even any county roads until 1910, and in some states even later. There were no signs with highway numbers along the roads because the state and federal numbering systems were a phenomenon of the 20s. Very few roads had names, except locally; that is, the road to such-and-such or such-and-such pike.

Third, there were few road signs. Seldom were there markers to indicate, at the junction of two pairs of muddy ruts, which pair of ruts should be followed because it was the highway. Finally, and most importantly, there wasn't enough economic push for creation of maps for automobile drivers. After all, no one knew whether cars would become anything more than just a fad, another toy for the rich. Few persons predicted that cars would become the dominant mode of transportation. Practically no one saw a future without railroads as the primary form of transportation. Most people assumed that personal transport would be by horseback. Similarly, few people could see much demand for road maps, and, without demand, map publishers would continue to market railroad maps and ignore the possibility of selling automobile road maps.

For a full half century, from the early 1920s through the first few years of the 1970s, the travel guides of choice were maps provided free of charge by gasoline dealers. The folding maps, showing either individual states or regions, first appeared in 1914. They were handy and, because they were free, most automobile glove boxes contained a few.

The arrival of the free maps distributed by gasoline companies coincided with the arrival of the gasoline filling station. In the days of relatively few automobiles, their drivers found it difficult to locate gasoline. Some general stores sold gasoline along with food and dry goods, and some repair garages and car dealers sold gasoline. But there were no large underground tanks from which to pump gasoline into cars; indeed, a single horseless carriage driver might buy a dealer's entire stock of gasoline at one time. As more and more automobiles were sold, demand for gasoline increased and stations were established for the sole purpose of selling gasoline.

**A Gulf station located on a major highway. Note the portable gasoline pump to the right. Caufield and Shook Convention, University of Louisville Photographic Archives.**

National Automotive History Collection, Detroit Public Library.

266

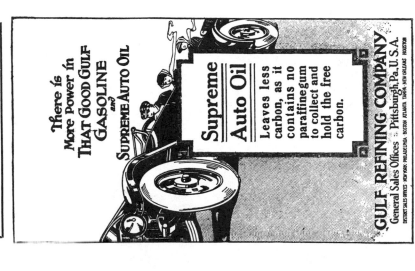

TOURING maps of New England, New York, New Jersey, Pennsylvania, Southern States, Middle West States, Texas and Transcontinental, showing all trails. Copies may be obtained from any of our dealers who display the Sign of the Orange Disc, or mailed on request. We maintain a touring bureau and cheerfully furnish touring information on request.

Early tri-fold map distributed by the Gulf Refining Company of Pittsburgh. Published by the Automobile Blue Book Publishing Company. This one was probably printed in 1915. 1917.

267

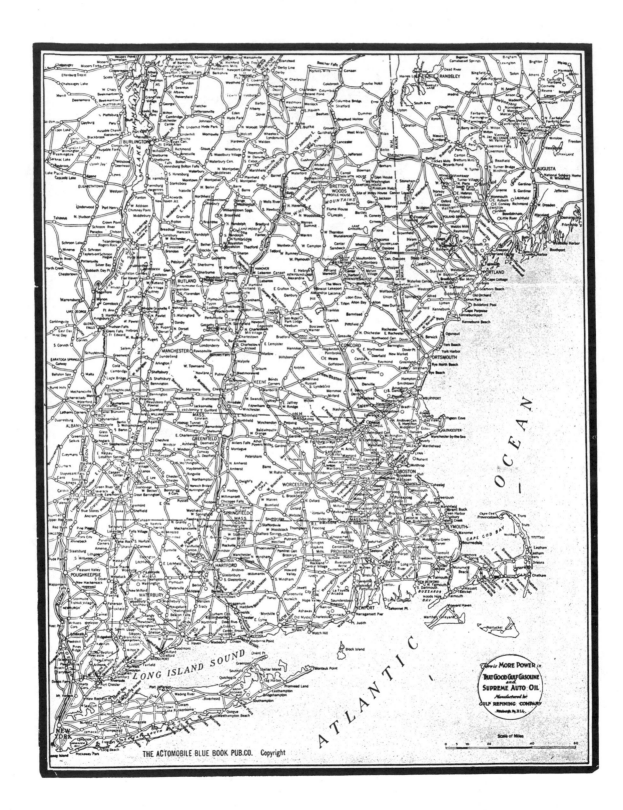

Apparently, it was the Gulf Refining Company which had the first road maps printed and then distributed the maps through gasoline dealers. Their first map was of Pennsylvania's Allegheny County (site of Pittsburgh), and 10,000 copies were sent by mail to advertise the opening of Gulf's first drive-in gasoline station. Maps of the entire states of New York, Pennsylvania, and New Jersey then were given away, some 300,000 of them, by Gulf service stations and dealers. And the idea was underway.

**Marguerite Rubel Collection.**

The chief competitor for earliest gasoline road maps was the Monarch Oil Refining Company on the West Coast. As early as 1912, Monarch sold a small booklet with 200 tiny maps and tourist information for fifty cents under the title of *Auto Road Maps for California and Nevada*. In 1914, Monarch copyrighted a large map intended to be placed on a wall, probably in service stations. Titled *General Automobile Roads of California, Nevada, Oregon, and Washington*, it noted locations of distributors of Monarch oils, greases, and gasoline.

The primary source of information for production of the oil company maps was, of course, state highway departments. Such organizations, of necessity,

**Early 1920s map of Florida, preceding the Tamiami Trail or any other road in southern Florida from the east coast to the west coast.**

had to keep accurate maps of their systems and construction in progress. Many states served the touring public by printing and distributing their own maps.

Among the companies that printed the maps distributed by oil companies, Rand McNally certainly was one of the pioneers. We know that they printed a map of Pennsylvania and Delaware, copyrighted in 1915, for the Atlantic Refining Company. Gulf's maps in the late teens were printed by the Automobile Blue Book Company, a major producer of guidebooks, which had separate maps inserted in a pocket in the back of the book. These could be removed and carried in the car while the large guidebook was left at home. Apparently, the same Blue Book maps were printed for Gulf to distribute at their gasoline stations. In the early 20s, Gulf maps became so popular that the company switched to Rand McNally, the country's largest map publisher, to produce their maps.

The Hammond Map Company, better known for their production of world globes and atlases, printed some of the early road maps. The General Drafting Company entered the oil company map field in 1923 when the Standard Oil Company of New Jersey ordered 280,000 maps of New Jersey. The H.M. Gousha Company, organized in 1926, soon became and remains a major producer of oil company maps and road atlases. Although they apparently did not produce oil company maps, the Clason Company of Denver produced many folding state maps, either to sell directly to tourists or for other types of companies to use for advertising.

**Portion of the official highway department road map of Oklahoma, 1925. Black lines indicate pavement, white indicate dirt roads. Pavement was in place near Tulsa and Oklahoma but one traveling between the state's two major cities traveled mostly on dirt roads.**

For a road map to be functional, there must be some obvious, visible relationship between a line on the map and the actual highway represented by that line. Today we think of highways in terms of numbers, and that system works well. The federal numbering system came into

271

**Long lines to buy gasoline are nothing new. Caufield and Shook Collection, University of Louisville Photographic Archives.**

being in November 1926, providing a consistent, nationwide numbering system. The American Association of State Highway Officials (AASHO) adopted the U.S. Numbered System for a group of important highways, about 90,000 miles worth. States had numbered their highways before this, but there were no consistent patterns, and numbers usually changed at a state line. Prior to the development of the Interstate system of highways, major cross country routes were designated as U.S. highways, even-numbered routes going east and west and odd-numbered routes going more-or-less north and south.

Another marking system, although not a governmentally financed one, was in place much earlier. Roads crossing several states were given names by booster groups, chambers of commerce, or highway associations. These groups intended to promote tourism through their communities by providing a means for "finding the way." Each named highway had a characteristic mark-

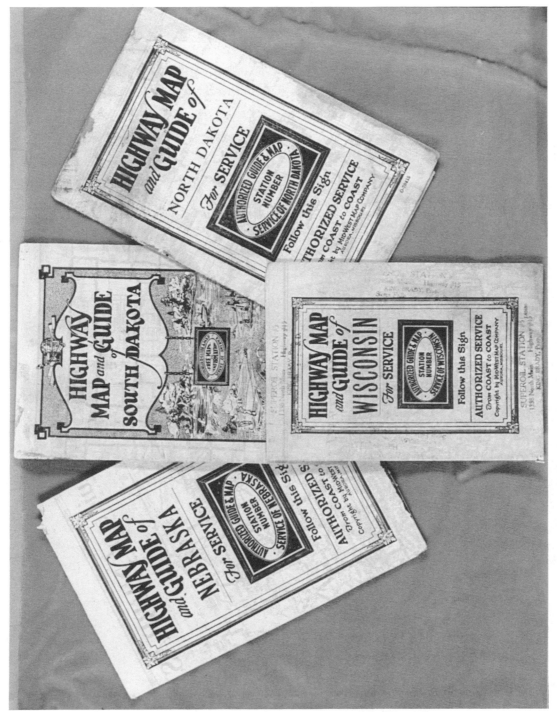

Four of the free maps distributed by stations associated with the Authorized Service organization.

ing, usually a grouping of colored stripes or geometric shapes. This made the job of following a road map a three-step affair, from name on the map to a legend to identify the marker and then observation of the marker as one drove. The numbering system eliminated the middle step, and numbers were quicker and easier to read than names. Of course, for the tourist, the three-step maps were a major improvement over reading a paragraph in a guidebook which described landmarks and gave distances between landmarks.

Organizations of businessmen and town boosters published guides for specific routes across the country. An effective means to advertise their named highway and to promote business in their cities was to provide a free guide book. Later, these groups printed free maps for distribution by member businesses along the route of the highway.

Republic truck dealership and a truck hauling part of the cotton harvest. Southwest Collection, El Paso Public Library A5507.

**1907 Pierce-Arrow serves as the vehicle for the Mount Hood Stage Line. Bill White collection.**

The National Midland Trail Association published a guidebook in 1916 under the title of *Tour Book, The Midland Trail, The Shortest Motor Road From Coast to Coast*. This guidebook had a dedication statement, the rhetoric of which is typical of the style of writing about early touring and the good roads movement of that time.

> To the cause of "GOOD ROADS EVERYWHERE," for the end that our United States shall be better equipped for the works of peace, better prepared for the fortunes of war, and that the sympathetic intercourse of her people shall make them truly one nation under one flag, with their common destiny and foremost purpose in all their hearts....
>
> To all the good men who are striving earnestly for the cause of Good Roads, and whose efforts are slowly realizing for us the

great things which Good Roads bring and which are our destiny....

To all Motor Tourists, in the hope that as time goes on they may travel over constantly bettering highways, with more open eyes, more receptive minds, and the most kindly desire to know their country and its people....

To all these people and purposes

THIS BOOK and the NATIONAL MIDLAND TRAIL ASSOCIATION for which it is made, are hopefully dedicated.

The "General Foreword" for the guidebook gives an excellent view of what it was like to tour by automobile just before World War I:

**Library of Congress.**

General Foreword

To tour by motor car in the United States today is not altogether a joyous performance, but the labor of such travel is more than repaid by the beauties to be seen, by the healthful nature of the pastime and by the knowledge of our institutions and our people which may be gained thru this mode of travel.

Any car in good shape mechanically, not overloaded with supplies and driven with ordinary care and consideration for its weaknesses as a machine, may with safety go anywhere East or West in our country today. To equip a car for such a trip, it is only necessary to have it in good repair, to provide tools for such repairs as may be made on the road, and with a coil of soft iron

**National Automotive History Collection, Detroit Public Library.**

wire, a good small shovel, an ax of small size, good tire chains, a light rope of steel wire 25 to 50 feet in length, a set of steel triple blocks and a steel pin an inch in diameter and three feet long, with a sharp point. These items of equipment should have permanent places provided about the car for carrying them and will be found useful quite as often in the East as in the West.

The traveler will find to his surprise that touring by motor in the West is just as apt on the whole to take him over passable roads as in the East and quite often that, there is much less bad or impassable road in the former region. Climatic conditions and character of soil are responsible for this, altho it is true that length of roads and wealth of country considered, the West gives far more care to its highways than does the country east of the Mississippi, and that some of the natural roadways of the mountains and prairies are as fine for comfortable travel as the paved ways of the East.

Tires, which are always somewhat of a problem, seem to be more so today than ever. It is well to be sure that the size with which the car is equipped is large enough to give a good margin of safety over the loading and weight of the car as ready for the trip. The using of a tire slightly oversize to give this margin is a good economy, provided it is not carried to extremes, for the oversize tire if too large makes heavy demands on the mileage-per-gallon figure. Unless the tires are of an odd size or make renewals may be obtained almost anywhere, and the spares which should be at least three tubes and two good casings (preferably new) ought to enable the traveler to arrive at some base of supplies even under the most unfortunate circumstances. Some sort of simple, efficient power pump is very desirable, to insure that tires will always carry the same and a sufficient air pressure.

While few motor car drivers have much knowledge of the mechanics of their cars, it is well to learn the adjustment of the carburetor as, especially in the mountains of the West, adjustments to changes in altitude are sometimes necessary, and are often quite desirable in the more humid air of the East. If the engine is known to perform better with some particular grade and weight of oil it is desirable to carry a reserve supply of this oil, and here it is well to note that generally speaking, the

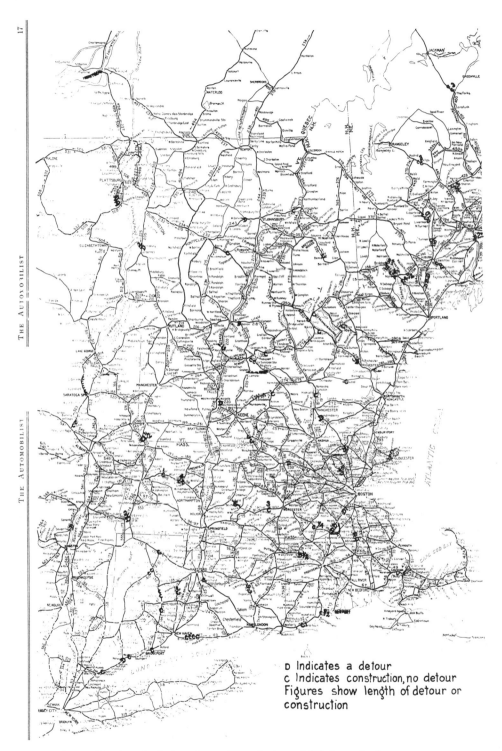

D Indicates a detour
C Indicates construction, no detour
Figures show length of detour or
construction

**A 1923 map of New England states from *The Automobilist* magazine.**

279

smaller towns of the West are apt to have garages better supplied and equipped than places of similar size in the East.

 While it is possible to make the trip and camp along the way, it is generally better not to burden any car with the weight of camping equipment, especially since good hotels may nearly always be reached at the end of the day's journey. And here again the tourist can look for very good accommodations at small places in the West, due to the fact that the native population of that section, being from the nature of their situation, accustomed to travel a good deal, demand and support good hotels and eating places. In passing it is well to note that hotels on the European plan are more general than in the East.

Local information is not always as reliable and complete as it should be, but in this book, thru the efforts of the National Midland Trail Association, it is attempted to maintain a headquarters of some sort in most of the towns on the Midland Trail (designated MTH) where reliable information may be obtained, and since in but few instances are any hotels or garages mentioned in the log. It is better on reaching a town to go direct to headquarters, there to be directed to accommodations.

Everyone is familiar with the maps, guidebooks, and other touring services offered by the Automobile Association of America, the "triple A." During the early years of the century, a number of other national and regional organizations were active and provided both maps and guides for members. One of these, The Automobile Legal Association, printed an excellent monthly magazine, called *The Automobilist*, for its members. It contained articles describing possible tours, places of scenic beauty to visit, camping hints, and road conditions in various locales. It also included regional or state maps showing construction sites, detours, and unusually bad roads. Even trade magazines, such as *Motor Age*, included travel information and stories about group travel.

Many of the organizations that privately designated highway routes by name and marked those routes belonged to the National Highways Association. The NHA's purpose was to promote the idea of a national system of highways and lobby for the federal government to build and maintain those highways. As early as 1914, this group proposed a group of routes which they believed to be an appropriate set of "national" highways for the entire country. Indeed, their proposed highway network was not too different from the grid of U.S. highways in place by 1930.

The switch in mode of travel from train to automobile came about, at least to a great extent, because cars could go where trains could not. They were not bound to a set of rails which took the most level, most direct route. As James P. Holland said as early as 1903 in "The Future of the Automobile": "Where the locomotive is hard bound to the narrow gauge of a carefully laid out and expensive road, the automobile is free to come and go by highways and byways, up hill and down dale, over stubble field or through morass, unhampered, free, and trustworthy as a faithful hound."

Though Holland wrote in the optimistic, over-zealous style of the time, automobiles indeed were not tied to an expensive pair of rails which simply could not go everywhere. In spite of the inhibition in auto sales and road building, which occurred during World War I, the teens and 20s were great years for the automobile industry and for road construction. Just as important for the drivers who would use auto and road, the evolution of maps and guidebooks had

**Gas station/cafe, Mercer County, Kentucky.**

proceeded by this time to the point that drivers could find out "how to get there."

Americans moved quickly to develop love affairs with the automobile and the road, particularly the open road. The opportunity to select a route and to have a variety of ways in which to go developed rapidly once federally supported road building began.

# 10
# *Signs of the Times*

**A** wide variety of signs and markers have been important to traveling automobilists from the beginning. Nearly as important as maps and guidebooks
were the indicators along the road, which identified the route and showed the

**Dixie Highway danger sign, 19.8 miles from Miami and 1,538.2 from Detroit. Florida State
Archives.**

283

driver which way to go. Indeed, maps and route instructions always had to relate to items visible and readily identifiable by the driver along the road or highway.

Landmarks such as trees, boulders, barns, telegraph poles, and buildings were cited in travel guides as proof that motorists were following a route correctly. Soon those were supplemented by markings deliberately placed. During the era of the named highways, a variety of marks were used. Some of these were as simple as blazes upon trees, no different from trail markings used by pioneers who traveled by foot or horseback. A significant portion of the Yellowstone Trail through sections of the plains of North and South Dakota, which

**Hupmobile dealership in El Paso, Texas. Southwest Collection, El Paso Public Library.**

**Sign erecting crew of the Automobile Club of Southern California. National Automotive History Collection, Detroit Public Library.**

**Ohio Historical Society.**

**Early Kentucky bus line. Roy L. Shannon Collection.**

were devoid of trees, was marked with large stones painted yellow. Many a touring group followed colored stripes around fence posts as they sought their way to a particular destination.

Not until after World War I was there any appreciable state effort in marking routes. Before that, travel associations such as the American Automobile Association or local member groups of the AAA and, more extensively, the named highway associations, put up the signs and markers that existed. In addition to signs on posts, the technique with which we are familiar, marks were painted on bridge abutments, culverts, buildings adjacent to roads, city lamp posts, trees and utility poles.

A major reason for developing a more sophisticated kind of marking was speed. As road quality improved, automobile quality improved, and the speed at which motorists traveled increased. Traveling at five or ten miles per hour, the motorist usually could search the countryside safely for landmarks designated in the route book. At a speed of twenty-five miles per hour the driver needed to focus attention more closely to the road. One could not let his or her eyes stray too far away from the right-of-way lest a curve be approached too rapidly or a soft spot in the road or a major bump come unobserved with unfortunate consequences. The higher speed meant that landmarks for finding one's way needed to be close to the road and easy to identify.

A second reason for improved route markings was the matter of increased traffic. In 1912, there were approximately a million automobiles on U.S. highways. A decade later there were nearly fifteen times that many. An article in the *Saturday Evening Post*, in August 1924, suggested that fifteen million Americans would indulge in some sort of automobile trip that year. "On a normal summer day 5000 tourist cars pause at our free tourist camp or buzz through east or west on the Lincoln Highway or north or south on the Meridian Highway," claimed the author of that article about his hometown of Rochelle, Illinois. All of those tourists made it to Rochelle following signs and

**Along with selling tires and distributing guidebooks, the B.F. Goodrich Company erected hundreds of road signs. University of Akron Archives.**

markers for the two famous named highways. So the markers worked. Yet it was time for a change in the way roads were designated and marked.

During World War I and immediately thereafter, it became obvious to the state highway engineers (or highway directors, depending upon terminology selected by the separate states) that a new and simple highway designation was needed. Quite a few stretches of designated state highways were not included as part of any named highway. And once the named highways reached their zenith during the mid-20s, some road maps were crowded with highway names. The legend for all the names required a great deal of space as well.

Numbers were the simple and obvious solution. Apparently, Wisconsin was the first state to develop state route markers and the numbered method for

"Tourist Bureau of the B.F. Goodrich Co. -- Route Books, Maps, etc. Free at Branches and Depots" according to signage on the side of the "Official Guide Post Truck." University of Akron Archives.

designating routes. Numbering not only simplified the situation for motorists, it was important to highway departments for recording expenditures, planning, and maintenance. Initially, the Wisconsin Highway Department did not erect special signs; it simply painted appropriate numbers on available poles, just as had been done with identifying marks for named highways.

**GOODRICH
ROAD SIGN**

Once the use of numbers to designate highways became standard practice by the states, the design of the markers became important. We are accustomed to fairly simple, rectangular signs for highway numbers, but earlier there were some rather artistic signs in use. A number of states employed the outline of the state map, including Missouri, Georgia, Arizona, Arkansas, and Ohio. Because such outlines were more expensive to cut out of sheet steel than were rectangles, a number of states used their outlines, but painted them upon a rectangular sign. Alabama, Indiana, Illinois, and Louisiana used such signs.

The most distinctive signs were those of Nebraska, New Mexico, and North Dakota, although the Kansas sunflower sign and the Utah beehive were pretty special, too. The three states, all beginning with the letter N, perhaps could employ their unusual and expensive-to-produce signs because they

**Typical appearance of a Goodrich sign as pictured on the cover of one of the Goodrich Route Books.**

Only text on Goodrich is on p. 255

**Stop in your Model T and buy groceries or gas from the Rhododendron Store in Oregon. Bill White collection.**

had fewer highways to mark. But the fewer highways covered many miles in the western plains. Nebraska displayed a covered wagon with a relatively small number. New Mexico used a round sign with the Zia symbol and a small number in the center. North Dakota superimposed a small number upon a profile view of an Indian chief. Each of these elaborate designs resulted in a much smaller number than was true for the average state highway sign, and the smaller numbers were more difficult to read at high speed.

Numbering state highways was a major step forward, but a consistency of numbers was needed for transcontinental trips or any trips of considerable distance. The American Association of State Highway Officials (AASHO) called for "immediate selection of transcontinental and interstate routes from the Federal Aid Road system, said roads to be continuously designated by means of standard highway marking signs...." In November 1926, the initial network of "federal" highways was approved with some 96,626 miles of highway. The shield was selected to mark the routes. Interestingly, it was voluntary action on the part of the chief state officials for highways that resulted in a uniform numbering system. Action by Congress or some federal agency was not necessary.

The more tourists there were on the road, the greater was the need for information for those tourists. The multiple signpost installation became common. At intersections or forks in a highway, a post was erected upon which were placed signs showing which route went where, what towns were to be found in various directions, and how far away those towns were. Indications of acceptable speed likewise were needed, as were signs pointing out dangers to travelers. Many of these kinds of signs were placed by the associations of automobile drivers and the named highway associations. But there was no more uniformity in distribution of signs than there was in the quality of roads from location to location. In some

locations, the distribution was scarce indeed. Following her coast-to-coast trip in 1915 (see page 259), etiquette expert Emily Post had this to say: "In the Middle West, automobile associations...do magnificent work. Roads are splendidly sign posted...." But among the great distances of the West, Ms. Post referred to "our road disappearing into hilly, roadless prairie." Through New Mexico, Arizona, and southern Colorado, directions usually had to be obtained from people rather than signs.

As the signing of highways first began, informational signs could consist of brief messages written out. A great deal of creativity and cleverness surfaced in signs, including attempts to frighten the motorist into careful driving. Again, as roads improved and automobile speed increased, there was a need for simple, universally and immediately understood symbols.

It was an organization of highway departments that recognized the need for uniformity in marking, responding to the rapid increase of interstate tourism. The Mississippi Valley Association of State Highway Departments, in 1922, established practice for its member states of using certain shapes for common signs. The idea of correlating a particular shape with a type of information originated with a maintenance engineer employed by the Wisconsin Highway Department -- J.T. Donaghey. The signs chosen were those we use today: the octagonal sign for stop, the diamond for caution because there may be a hazard in the road, the rectangle for information, and the crossbuck for railroad crossings.

The annual Convention Proceedings for 1924 of the American Road Builders Association, an organization of road contractors, reported on the need for uniform warning and caution signs. "Other states will do well to fall in line and adopt this system [that of the Mississippi Valley Association] of warning signs. The sooner a system of warning signs is standardized the country over, the sooner will there be a noticeable decrease in highway traffic accidents."

Another organization, the American Association of State Highway Officials, took up the cause in 1924, recommending adoption of uniform signing prac-

**American Automobile Association's recommendations for standardized signs, circa 1920.**

tices. At the same time that the AASHO recognized the need for a nationwide numbering system, the group studied the matter of safety and informational signs. How much better it would be for the tourist if there was consistency of signs from state to state. Based upon the Mississippi Valley system, the AASHO recommendations added color coordination: red for stop and yellow for caution. Again, the automobile organizations played a role as the sign recommendations of the American Automobile Association preceded those of the highway officials.

The first stop signs for traffic control were employed by the city of Detroit in 1915. Use of the stop signs created, at the same time, the first routes through a city which had the right-of-way over intersecting streets. It seems particularly appropriate that traffic control techniques would originate in the automotive capital.

The Denver Motor Club may well have placed the most unusual kind of warning sign ever used along highways. West of Denver were (and are) roads into mountain areas with magnificent scenery of great interest to travelers from near and far. Early mountain highways had very sharp curves, some so sharp that drivers had to swing into the curve, then back up and "jockey" around it. The *Denver Post* reported in 1916 that the Denver Motor Club had made travel safer: "In order that motorists on the Bear Creek Canyon Road may see approaching machines in both directions, on one side of the most dangerous curves two large mirrors have been erected."

Among the leaders who influenced early highway development, Carl G. Fisher must come near the top of the list. An entrepreneur who was very much involved in the automobile business as owner of the Prest-O-Lite Company, Fisher is known today as the father of both the idea for a transcontinental highway and the Lincoln Highway. Fisher dreamed of a highway from New York to San Francisco to be called the "Ocean to Ocean Rock Highway."

**From the collections of Henry Ford Museum and Greenfield Village.**

Pathfinder car on the Lincoln Highway. National Automotive History Collection, Detroit Public Library.

Fisher's own comment about the idea was: "A road across the United States; Let's build it before we're too old to enjoy it."

Fisher's Prest-O-Lite company made a major contribution to night driving before the days of electric headlights. His company made pressurized tanks to supply acetylene gas to auto headlamps. And, of course, he founded the granddaddy of all automobile race tracks, the Indianapolis Speedway.

The Lincoln Highway, or more correctly, the Lincoln Memorial Highway, was, and still is, among those who remember the named highways, the best known road of the 1920s. Sometimes it is referred to as the first of the named highways, but it does not deserve that honor. Although not the oldest named highway, it certainly was the most influential. Both the organization created around the movement to construct the highway, with formation of a national association, and the style of construction used, served as models for other highways. Another important auto pioneer joined Fisher in the early leadership of the Lincoln Highway project, Henry Joy, president of the Packard Motor Car Company.

From the beginning, directors of the Lincoln Memorial Highway Association were committed to finding the route for the road which would be the shortest, most direct, most usable throughout the year, and least costly to build. Of course, planners faced a tremendous barrier of mountains when they came to

**Colorado Historical Society.**

**Nebraska farm wife routinely starts her Model T Ford, the hard way. Photo courtesy Dena Schulke.**

Colorado. To skirt the mountains to the south would take the road across Arizona and Southern California, where sand and extremely high temperatures through several months of the year would make travel difficult in open cars. To go north would bring winter problems of snow and ice. The route selected was announced to the Conference of Governors in August 1913; it proceeded west from Cheyenne, Wyoming, through the flattest area available in the Rocky Mountain chain. The original route, New York to San Francisco, was 3,389 miles. Subsequent revisions brought the distance down to 3,143 miles.

Getting such a massive project going, with no government involvement and before mechanized road building equipment was available, was a tremendous undertaking. Since the vast majority of citizens still traveled by horseback and railroad at the time, a tremendous amount of motivating was essential. A caravan tour to promote the concept was organized in July 1913 in Indianapolis. Seventeen autos and two trucks made the journey from there westward to Los Angeles without serious mishap, but the trip required thirty-four days and was not completed without serious struggle. Berthoud Pass west of Denver was a steep climb on rough roads intended for horses and wagons. Some cars had to turn around and back up the road because the incline made carburetors higher than the gasoline tanks which fed them.

Another problem for the highway-advertising caravan had nothing to do with car or road. At one place where the group stopped for the night, Carl Fisher said, "I do believe they have the biggest bed bugs in the world." Some of the bedbugs were alleged to be so large that a sleepy motorist, awakening in semidarkness, saw "a mandolin hanging on the wall above him, smashed it with a chair and vowed that, seeing it move, he had mistaken it for one of the night's too numerous companions."

Early travelers on the highway didn't necessarily enjoy it. Emily Post had a strong opinion she expressed in *By Motor to the Golden Gate*:

> Thirty-six miles out of Chicago we met the Lincoln Highway and from the first found it a disappointment. As the most important, advertised and lauded road in our country, its first appearance was not engaging. If it were called the cross continent trail you would expect little, and be philosophical...you wake rather unhappily to the actuality of a meandering dirt road that becomes mud half a foot deep after a day or two of rain!
>
> Still we went over it easily enough until we passed DeKalb. After that the only "highway" attributes left were the painted red, white, and blue signs decorating the telegraph poles along the way. The highway itself disappeared into a wallow of mud! The center of the road was slightly turtle-backed; the sides were of thick, black ooze and ungaugedly deep, and the car was possessed, as though it were alive, to pivot around and slide backward into it.... If the Lincoln Highway was like this what would the ordinary road be [?]

Although he deserves a great deal of credit, Fisher's Lincoln Highway was not the first of the great named highways that ran through at least several states, although it became the best known. Indeed, it is difficult to designate a first.

In the history of the automobile, backyard mechanics all over the country put together motorized buggies, which functioned at least to some degree. Similarly highway projects sprang up independently all around the country. During the late teens and the 1920s, a great movement spread across the country to organize businesses, chambers of commerce and booster groups from cities and towns along logical routes into highway associations. Some of the individual movements lived, some died, but all helped in the campaign to get better roads.

Perhaps the most important contribution of the named highway movement was getting people who lived many, many miles from one another concerned about quality of roads over a significant distance. Typical travelers in 1910, or 1915 for that matter, could drive for a few miles on reasonably good roads and then, as they crossed a county line, encounter nothing but impassable mud and ruts. Analysis of highways in almost any state revealed a checkerboard of good and bad roads, county by county. This was caused by the fact that the responsibility for road work initially was with the county (or even township where that was a unit of local government). Without the impetus provided by the private highway organizations, the patchwork condition of roads no doubt would have continued much longer.

Probably the first of the great highway organizations to have some sort of formal organization was the Yellowstone Trail, organized at Lemmon, South Dakota, in October 1911. At least some South Dakotans claim that the "first"

**Kentucky Historical Society.**

299

highway was initiated in their state, although what was planned in 1911 was not yet a cross-country road. In a July 1924 issue of *The Outlook*, in an article on "Autocamping -- the Fastest Growing Sport," author Brimmer referred to the three first cross-country trips by auto in 1903, and the highways to follow: "...still no bona fide transcontinental highway was opened until nine years later. This was the Yellowstone Trail, established in October, 1912 [actually 1911]. One year later the Lincoln Highway was founded."

Actual construction started on the Yellowstone Trail considerably before any earth was moved for the Lincoln Highway. A group of men started grading and preparing the road near Aberdeen, South Dakota, during the week of July 11, 1912, even before any money was provided by either the association or counties through which the road would run. Enthusiasts then decided to build, that summer, a two-mile stretch which would serve as a sample for the rest of the highway. By April 1914, the route was firm from Minneapolis to Yellowstone. And in July of that year, three cars traveled the entire length of the highway as it then existed.

On Jan. 19, 1915, the Twin Cities-Aberdeen-Yellowstone Park Association determined to extend its highway from coast to coast, the eventual route being from Seattle through Billings, Montana; Aberdeen, South Dakota; to the Twin Cities; Chicago; and finally to Plymouth, Massachusetts.

On one of their earliest (hand drawn) maps, the Yellowstone Trail Association published an interesting slogan: "Stick to the Yellowstone Trail -- When it is bad we will tell you." A major effort to advertise the road was made by attempting to run a relay from Chicago to Seattle in 1915, hopefully in 100 hours. Twenty-one different cars and drivers participated, making the run in ninety-seven hours and ten minutes. The most difficult section of the relay was through the Standing Rock Indian Reservation in South Dakota. Rains had muddied much of the route, and the driver of this section became hopelessly stuck in a mud hole during the middle of a cloudy night. With no help available, he ran to McLaughlin, some three miles, and got two automobiles to go back with him and pull his car out of the mud hole.

The president of the association was to ride with the drivers on the first several legs of the relay between Chicago and Minneapolis, but one enthusiastic driver took off without the association's leader, stranding him in a strange town. A symbolic letter from the Chicago mayor to the Seattle mayor was delivered in only four days, but one person who failed to catch the vision of the relay said, "Why go to all this trouble when you can send the damned letter for two cents?"

Literally hundreds of other routes were laid out and named by private groups without benefit of government funds. A 1947 volume, titled *Wisconsin Highways*, said:

> From 1911 to 1917, there was an epidemic of unofficial laying out and marking of routes for through travel by promotional organizations. The movement probably had its origin in Iowa in 1911 and spread throughout the United States. In Wisconsin the first trail laid out and marked was the Lake to River Road from Milwaukee to Madison to Prairie du Chien and to La Crosse. Thereafter, additional trails were laid out and marked, such as the Yellowstone Trail, the Black and Yellow Trail, the Grant Trail, the Red Ball Trail, and numerous other routes of other designations.
>
> As there was no restraint on the number of trails that could be laid out, many were routed over roads that it was most inadvisable to travel.

No doubt the latter statement was true but, in many states, to find roads already built which were "advisable" to travel simply was not possible. For example, it was in 1912 that Idaho "covered the mud" with its first few miles of graveled road, and in 1918 celebrated the achievement of some five miles of paved highway.

While the Yellowstone Trail and Lincoln Highways were east-west routes, probably the best known named highway with a north-south orientation was the Dixie Highway. In a story titled "'tucky in the Mud" in the *American Motorist* for July 1951, C. Frank Dunn said:

> The first effort to get through roads across the state was launched on paper in 1915, when the Dixie Highway, from Michigan to Miami, was projected. The late Capt. W.S. Gilbreath announced that a meeting of representatives of all towns between Chicago and Miami, by way of Indianapolis, Louisville, Chattanooga and Atlanta, would be held in Chattanooga, and the Governors of the states through which the trunk thoroughfare was to pass were invited....
>
> But getting the name did not get the highway, as there was no one and no organization to build it. That was before there was a State Highway Department, or even a Federal Bureau of Public Roads.

Trouble at the railroad crossing. New Mexico Highway Department.

New Mexico Highway Department.

This was not quite accurate because the highway department in Kentucky was founded in 1912, and although there was not a Bureau of Public Roads until 1918, its predecessor organization, the Office of Public Roads and Rural Engineering, was alive and well.

Getting the name certainly did not get the highway, as described by a traveler over the Dixie "highway" in 1919: "The road to the mountain is indescribable, being half boulders two feet in diameter, and the balance thick, red sticky mud."

The names for highways ran the gamut of creativity. Some bore historical names because their routes followed major wagon roads of the Old West. The Santa Fe Trail was such a route, and it was not long before there were two of them, the old and the new Santa Fe Trails. Then there was the Custer Battlefield Highway. Other names were as simple as colors used to mark the

Cover of a free map of Nebraska roads of 1924, distributed by Standard Oil Company, maker of Red Crown Gasoline.

way: the Golden Belt, the Red Line, the White Way, the Blue Line, and the Black and Yellow Trail. Some, like the Lincoln Highway, bore the names of famous people, including the Carrie Nation Highway. Still others had geographical identification in their names: the North and South Pike, the Short Cut West Highway, the Black Hills-Devils Lake Highway, or the Lakes to Gulf Highway. This last unit, a road from Duluth to Galveston, demonstrated the level of interest in some of the highways when more than 1200 representatives attended a convention for that road in 1922.

Each road had a specific identification, as simple in some cases as colored stripes around fence posts and telephone poles. Signs bearing an identifying symbol were tacked up along routes, an oil well derrick for the Oil Belt Route or an appropriately chosen hatchet for the Carrie Nation Highway.

Initially, those persons who wanted to develop highways were concerned about their own potential travel. But it was not long before the motivation

**Colorado Historical Society.**

behind named highway development became commercial in intent. Tourism became quite important to the economy of towns along named routes. One booster put it this way: "Our experience, and the experience of other states, is that the tourist industry is one of the most reliable and the most lucrative of all industries, and one which has grown exceptionally fast in the immediate past. Its future is most bright. People will travel."

And travel they did! They did so in greater and greater numbers every year, demanding better highways upon which to travel. With the erection of appropriate signs along the highways and placement of numbers upon maps, the method for finding one's way was complete. There was no excuse for getting lost any more. American automobile owners established themselves as the world's greatest tourists, but their autos provided only half of what was necessary to travel. The other half was the road -- dirt, mud, dust, rutted, rough or a ribbon of smooth concrete -- yet absolutely essential.

**Denver Public Library, Western History Collection.**

# Bibliography

## Books, monographs

*A Great Name in Oil.* New York: F. W. Dodge Co./McGraw Hill. Copyright Sinclair Oil Co., 1966.

Agg, Thomas R. *The Construction of Roads and Pavements.* New York: McGraw Hill, 1916.

Allhands, J. L. *Tools of the Earthmover -- Yesterday and Today.* Huntsville, TX: Sam Houston College Press, 1951.

Anderson, Andrew P. *Modern Road Building and Maintenance.* Chicago: Hercules Powder Co., 1920.

Anderson, Rudolph E. *The Story of the American Automobile.* Washington: Public Affairs Press, 1950.

Anderson, Scott. *Check the Oil: A Pictorial History of the American Filling Station.* Lombard, IL: Wallace-Homestead, 1986.

Arnold, Horace L. and Fay L. Faurote. *Ford Methods and the Ford Shops.* New York: Engineering Magazine Company, 1915.

The Association of Licensed Automobile Manufacturers. *Handbook of Gasoline Automobiles, 1904-1906.* New York: Dover, 1969.

*Automobile Blue Book.* Section No. 2, New England. New York: Automobile Blue Book Publishing Co., 1907.

*Automobile Blue Book.* Vol. 1, New York and Canada. New York: Automobile Blue Book Publishing Co., 1916.

Baker, Ira O. *A Treatise on Roads and Pavements.* New York: Wiley, 1903.

Balcomb, Kenneth C. *The Red River Hill.* Albuquerque, NM: Albuquerque Historical Society, 1981.

Balshone, Bruce L., Paul L. Deering, and Brian D. McCarl. *Bicycle Transit, Its Planning and Design.* New York: Praeger, 1975.

Belasco, Warren J. *Americans on the Road: From Autocamp to Motel, 1910-1945.* Cambridge: MIT Press, 1979.

Brown, Cecil K. *The State Highway System of North Carolina.* Chapel Hill, NC: University of North Carolina Press, 1931.

*The Camino Real.* Santa Fe, NM: The State Highway Commission [of New Mexico], 1915.

Cleveland, Reginald M. and S. T. Williamson. *The Road is Yours: The Story of the Automobile and the Men Behind It.* New York: Greystone, 1951.

Clymer, Floyd. *Treasury of Early American Automobiles, 1877-1925.* New York: Bonanza, 1950, particularly "Glidden Tours."

Collier, Peter and David Horowitz. *The Fords: An American Epic.* New York: Summit Books, 1987.

Cohn, David L. *Combustion on Wheels.* Boston: Houghton Mifflin, 1944.

Cracco, James. *History of the South Dakota Highway Department, 1919-1941.* Unpub. thesis, University of South Dakota, 1970.

Cranmer, H. Jerome. *New Jersey in the Automobile Age: A History of Transportation.* Princeton, NJ: D. Van Nostrand, 1964.

Diel, Charles. *Missouri Highways.* Jefferson City, MO: Missouri Highway Department, 1940.

Donovan, Frank. *Wheels for a Nation.* New York: Thomas Y. Crowell, 1965.

*Eighth Biennial Report, Department of State Lands, Highways, and Improvements.* Little Rock, AR: State of Arkansas, 1928.

*Federal Aid to Good Roads*, Report of the Joint Commission on Federal Aid in the Construction of Post Roads. Washington: House Documents, 63rd Congress, Third Session, vol. 99, 1915.

Flagg, Ernest. *Roads and Pavements.* New York: DeVinne Press, 1910.

Flink, James J. *America Adopts the Automobile, 1895-1910.* Cambridge: MIT Press, 1970.

_____ . *The Car Culture.* Cambridge: MIT Press, 1971.

_____ . *The Automobile Age.* Cambridge: MIT Press, 1988.

*First Biennial Report to the Governor and General Assembly.* Frankfort, KY: Department of Public Roads, Commonwealth of Kentucky, 1912.

Frost, H. *The Art of Roadmaking,* New York: Engineering News Publishing Co., 1910.

*Goodrich Long Island Route Book.* Akron, OH: The B. F. Goodrich Company, 1912.

Goodwin, Marion. *Our Alfalfa County Heritage, 1893-1976.* Cherokee, OK: Alfalfa County Historical Society, 1976.

Guillet, Edwin C. *The Story of Canadian Roads.* Toronto: University of Toronto Press, 1966.

Haworth, B. Smith. *Born Barefooted.* Lawrence, KS: Allen Press, 1969.

*Highways Handbook.* Washington: Highway Education Board, 1929.

Hill, F. E. *The Automobile, How It Came, Grew and Has Changed Our Lives.* New York: Dodd Mead and Co., 1967.

*History of the Tennessee Highway Department.* Nashville: Tennessee State Highway Department and the U.S. Department of Commerce, Bureau of Public Roads, 1959.

Holt, W. Stull. *The Bureau of Public Roads, Its History, Activities and Organization.* Baltimore: Johns Hopkins Press, 1923.

Hopley, John E. *History of Crawford County, Ohio.* Chicago: Richmond-Arnold Publishing Co., 1912.

Huebinger, M. *Iowa Official Transcontinental Route.* Des Moines, IA: Iowa Publishing Co., 1912.

Hulbert, Archer B. *The Future of Road-making in America*, vol. 15 of Historic Highways of America. New York: AMS Press, 1905.

Jacoby, J. Wilbur, ed. *History of Marion County, Ohio and Representative Citizens*. Chapter X Manufacturing and Commercial Enterprises of Marion. Marion, OH: Unigraphic and Marion County Historical Society, 1976 reprint, original printing 1907.

Jackson, Judith. *Man and the Automobile: A Twentieth Century Love Affair*. New York: McGraw Hill, 1979.

Jenkins, James T. Jr. *The Story of Roads*. Washington: American Road Builders Association, 1967.

Jennison, Peter S. *Roadside History of Vermont*. Missoula, MT: Mountain Press Publishing Co., 1989.

Johnson, A. E. *AASHO The First Fifty Years 1914-1964*. Washington: American Association of State Highway Officials, 1965.

Jordan, Philip D. *The National Road*. Indianapolis: Bobbs-Merrill, 1948.

Karolevitz, Robert F. *This Was Trucking*. New York: Bonanza, 1966.

_____ . *This Was Pioneer Motoring*. Seattle: Superior Publishing Co., 1968.

Kendrick, Baynard. *Florida Trails to Turnpikes 1914-1964*. Talahassee, FL.

Kimes, Beverly R. and Richard Langworth. *Packard: A History of the Motor Car and the Company*. Automobile Quarterly Publications, 1978.

Knowles, Ruth S. *The First Pictorial History of the American Oil and Gas Industry 1859-1983*. Athens, OH: Ohio University Press, 1983.

Labatut, Jean and Wheaton J. Lane, eds. *Highways in Our National Life, A Symposium*. Princeton, NJ: Princeton University Press, 1950.

Lacey, Robert. *Ford The Men and the Machine*. Boston: Little, Brown and Co., 1986.

Lancaster, Samuel C. *The Columbia, America's Great Highway*. Portland: Samuel Christopher Lancaster, 1915.

Larson, T. A. *History of Wyoming*. Lincoln, NE: University of Nebraska Press, 1965.

Lewis, David L. *The Public Image of Henry Ford*. Detroit: Wayne State University Press, 1976.

*The Lincoln Highway*. Binghampton, NY: Lincoln Highway Association, 1935.

Lynd, Robert S. and Helen M. *Middletown*. New York: Harcourt, Brace, 1929.

_____ . *Middletown in Transition*. New York: Harcourt, Brace, 1937.

Mason, Philip P. *The League of American Wheelmen and the Good Roads Movement, 1880-1905*. Ann Arbor, MI: University of Michigan Press, 1958.

_____ . *A History of American Roads*. Chicago: Rand McNally, 1967.

*Mato Paha, Land of the Pioneers*. Northwest Meade County: Alkali Community Club, 1969.

Maxim, Hiram P. *Horseless Carriage Days*. New York: Harper, 1936.

McCallie, S. W. *A Preliminary Report on the Roads and Road-Building Materials of Georgia*. Atlanta: Geological Survey of Georgia, Bulletin No. 8, 1901.

*Mendenhall's Guide and Road Map of Pennsylvania*. Cincinnati: C. S. Mendenhall, 1905.

*The Midland Trail Tour Book*. Glorietta, NM: Rio Grande Press, 1969, originally published Grand Junction, CO: Midland Trail Log Book Company, 1916.

Musselman, Morris M. *Get a Horse!* Philadelphia: J. B. Lippincott, 1950.

Myers, Dana W. *Snapshots, Waitsfield, Vermont, 1789-1989 Bicentennial.* Waitsfield, VY: Iota Press, 1989.

Nevins, Allan with Frank E. Hill. *Ford: The Times, the Man, the Company.* New York: Scribner's, 1954.

_____ . *Ford: Expansion and Challenge, 1915-1933.* New York: Scribner's, 1957.

Oppel, Frank, ed. *Motoring in America: The Early Years.* Secaucus, NJ: Castle Books, 1989.

Partridge, Bellamy. *Fill 'er Up: The Story of Fifty Years of Motoring.* New York: McGraw-Hill, 1952.

Patton, Phil. *Open Road: A Celebration of the American Highway.* New York: Simon & Schuster, 1986.

Poole, Ernest. *Nurses on Horseback.* New York: Macmillan, 1932.

Post, Emily. *By Motor to the Golden Gate.* New York: Appleton, 1916.

Rae, John B. *The American Automobile: A Brief History.* Chicago: University of Chicago Press, 1965.

_____ . *The Road and Car in American Life.* Cambridge: MIT Press, 1971.

Raine, James W. *Saddlebag Folk: The Way of Life in the Kentucky Mountains.* Evanston, IL: Row, Peterson, 1942.

Robinson, Elwyn B. *History of North Dakota.* Lincoln, NE: University of Nebraska Press, 1966.

Robinson, John. *Highways and Our Environment.* New York: McGraw Hill, 1974.

Romine, Trella H., ed. *Marion County 1979 History.* Marion, OH: Marion County Historical Society, 1979.

Rose, Albert C. *Historic American Highways.* Washington: American Association of State Highway Officials, 1953.

Scharff, Virginia. *Taking the Wheel: Women and the Coming of the Motor Age.* New York: Free Press, 1991.

Schroeder, Joseph J. Jr. *The Wonderful World of Automobiles, 1895-1930.* Chicago: Follett Publishing Co., 1971.

Seely, Bruce E. *Building the American Highway System: Engineers as Policy Makers.* Philadelphia: Temple University Press, 1987.

Snider, L. C. *Preliminary Report on the Road Materials and Road Conditions of Oklahoma.* Norman, OK: Bulletin no. 8, Oklahoma Geological Survey, 1911.

Sloan, Alfred P. Jr. *My Years with General Motors.* Garden City, NY: Doubleday, 1964.

Smith, Dwight A. *Columbia River Highway Historic District.* Nomination of the Old Columbia River Highway in the Columbia Gorge to the National Register of Historic Places. Eugene, OR: Oregon Department of Transportation, 1984.

Sorensen, Lorin. *The American Ford.* St. Helena, CA: Silverado, 1975.

Stern, Philip Van Doren. *Tin Lizzie: The Story of the Fabulous Model T Ford.* New York: Simon and Schuster, 1955.

Tucker, James I. *The American Road.* Norman, OK: University of Oklahoma Press, 1916.

Verhoeff, Mary. *The Kentucky Mountains, Transportation and Commerce. Vol. 1.* Louisville: John P. Morton Co., Publication 26 of the Filson Club, 1911.

Vieyra, Daniel I. *"Fill 'er Up", An Architectural History of America's Gas Stations.* New York, Macmillan, 1979.

Waynick, Capus. *North Carolina Roads and Their Builders*. Raleigh, NC: Superior Stone Co., 1952.

Wik, Reynold M. *Henry Ford and Grass-roots America*. Ann Arbor, MI: University of Michigan Press, 1972.

*Wisconsin Highways: A History of Wisconsin Highway Development 1835-1945*. Madison, WI: State Highway Commission and Public Roads Administration of Wisconsin, 1947.

Wixom, Charles W. *ARBA Pictorial History of Roadbuilding*. Washington: American Road Builders' Association, 1975.

## Articles, pamphlets, book chapters by author

Andrew, Col. H. R. "The Romance of the Nail-Picker." *New Mexico Highway Journal* (December 1930), vol. 8, no. 12.

Athearn, Robert G. "The Tin Can Tourists' West." In Rex C. Myers and Harry W. Fritz. *Montana and the West: Essays in Honor of K. Ross Toole*. Boulder, CO: Pruett Publishing Co., 1984.

Bartlett, F. L. "The History of Road Building in Colorado." *Colorado Highways Bulletin* (August 1918), vol. 1, no. 3.

Bennett, N. W. "Highway History in New Mexico." *New Mexico* (June 1932), vol. 10, no. 6.

Bowlby, H. L. "History of Road Building." *Colorado Highways* (November 1922), vol. 1, no. 11.

Brimmer, Frank E. "Autocamping -- the Fastest-Growing Sport." *The Outlook* (July 11, 1924), vol. 137, no. 11.

Bruce, William L. "Hard Surfaced Roads." *Pahasapa Quarterly* (April 1919) vol. 8, no. 3.

Brunskill, Virginia. "Clyde Raymond England." In *Proving Up: Jones County History*. Murdo, SD: Book and Thimble Club, 1969.

Butler, John L. "The Nail Picker, A TTT Truck." *Vintage Ford* (September-October 1982), vol. 17, no. 5.

_____ . "Model T's in Construction." *Vintage Ford* (September-October 1986), vol. 21, no. 5.

Buzzell, Francis M. "The Building of Roads by Convict Labor." *Popular Mechanics*, (1909), vol. 12.

_____ . "Rejuvenating Macadam Roads with Oil." *Popular Mechanics* (1911), vol. 15, no. 1.

Cooley, H. O. and J. W. Parmley. "Report on 'Chicago to Seattle over the Yellowstone Trail in 100 Hour' Run." Advertising flyer for the Yellowstone Trail Association.

Crosby, Maj. W. W. "Definitions Proposed for Terms Used in Highway Work." *Good Roads* (May 3, 1913), vol. V, no. 18.

Earle, H. S. "Roads: Yesterday, Today and Tomorrow." *Good Roads* (February 1911), vol. XII, no. 2.

Eblen, Elizabeth S. "Touring -- 1916 Style." *New Mexico* (May 1959), vol. 37, no. 5.

Findlay, William. "Signing the Highway." *Georgia Highways* (December 1926), vol. 4.

French, James A. *First and Second Reports of the State Engineer of New Mexico*. Santa Fe, NM: State of New Mexico, 1914 and 1916.

Fuller, Wayne E. "Good Roads and Rural Free Delivery of Mail." *Missouri Valley Historical Review* (1956), vol. XLII.

Gilbert, Helen M. "Plank Road Over the Sands of Algodones." *Desert Magazine* (February 1962), vol. 25, no. 2.

Gilbreath, W. S. "Government's Duty to Build Great Highway." *Indianapolis Sun*, Dec. 21, 1913.

Gross, Howard H. "Highways and Civilization." In *Modern Road Building*, Transactions of the First Congress of American Road Builders. St. Paul, MN: West Publishing Co., 1911.

Hafen, LeRoy R. "The Coming of the Automobile and Improved Roads to Colorado." *Colorado Magazine* (January 1931), vol. VIII, no. 1.

Harrison, Gen. E. G. "For Better Roads." *The Traders' Exchange and Commercial Club News* (November 1900), vol. 1, no. V.

Hataway, Marsha. "The Development of the Mississippi State Highway System, 1916-32." *Journal of Mississippi History* (1966), vol. 28, no. 4.

Interrante, Joseph. "The Road to Autopia: The Automobile and the Spatial Transformation of American Culture." In David L. Lewis, ed. *The Automobile and American Culture*. Ann Arbor, MI: Michigan Quarterly Review special issue (Fall, 1980, and Winter, 1981) vol. XIX, no. 4 and vol. XX, no. 1.

Isabella, N. M. "Highway Traffic Accidents -- Their Classification and Causes." In Robert K. Tomlin, Jr., ed. *Convention Proceedings*, American Road Builders Association, 1924.

Jensen, Louis J. "Ninety-one Years in South Dakota." In Eastern *Pennington County Memories*. Wall, SD: American Legion Auxiliary, 1965.

Kelly, B. F. "An Electro-Magnetic Nail-Picker for Freeing Highways of Metal Objects." *New Mexico Highway Journal* (March 1928), vol. VI.

_____. "A New High-Speed Maintainer." *New Mexico Highway Journal* (January 1929), vol. VII, no. 1.

Kendall, Charles P. "The Old Plank Road." *Antique Automobile* (March-April 1974), vol. 38, no. 2.

Kilgore, John. "Building a Road Across the Sea." In *Facts and Figures on Florida's Highways*. Tallahassee, FL: Florida State Road Department, reprinted from Florida Highways Magazine, August 1944.

Lampton, William J. "The Meaning of the Automobile." *Outing* (September 1902), vol. 40, no. 5.

Libby, Steve. "Across the Country in 61 Days." *Denver Post Empire Magazine*, Dec. 16, 1951.

May, Earl Chapin. "The Argonauts of the Automobile." *Saturday Evening Post* (Aug. 9, 1924), vol. 197, no. 5.

Michaelis, Bob. "Splinters Off the Plank Road." *Buckskin Bulletin* (Fall, 1983), vol, XVII, no. 4.

Page, Frank. "The Year's Work and Problems Ahead." In Robert K. Tomlin, ed. *Convention Proceedings, 21st Annual Convention*. Washington: American Road Builders Association, 1924.

Parris, John. "How Old Roads Were Engineered." *Asheville Citizen*, July 6, 1959.

_____ . "Winding Stairs Road Is Tribute to Sandlin." *Asheville Citizen*, April 22, 1963.

_____ . "Hacking Out Roads with Pick and Shovel." *Asheville Citizen.* Aug. 1, 1975.

Paxson, Frederic L. "The Highway Movement, 1916-1935." *American Historical Review* (January 1946), vol. LI, no. 2.

Peck, Frank S. "Roads; Past, Present and Future." *Pahasapa Quarterly* (April 1919), vol. VIII, no. 3.

Pope, Albert A. "Highway Improvement." Address before the Carriage Builders' National Association, Oct. 17, 1889.

Potter, Isaac B., Chairman, Committee on Improvement of the Highways, League of American Wheelmen, personal letter to Honorable N. P. Banks, Congressman from Massachusetts, Aug. 12, 1890.

Pratt, Charles E. "A Sketch of American Bicycling and its Founder." *Outing* (July 1891), vol. 18.

Rew, George C. "From Chicago to the Coast." *Motor* (December 1909), vol. 7, no. 3.

Rightmire, E. D. "'Meadow Roads' as Constructed in Southern New Jersey Counties." *Good Roads* (March 1911), vol. XII, no. 3.

Ristow, Walter W. "American Road Maps and Guides." *Scientific American* (May 1946), vol. 74, no. 5.

_____ . "A Half Century of Oil-Company Road Maps." *Surveying and Mapping* (December 1964), vol. 24, no. 4.

Rogers, Frank F. "Building Roads for the Nation." *Georgia Highways* (July 1926), vol. 4.

Scurr, K. R. "Old Forest City Bridge" and "New Bridges." In Cece and Ruth Stilgebouer, eds. *Gettysburg 75th Anniversary.* Pierre, SD: State Publishing Co., 1958.

Sherwell, Guillermo A. "The Economic and Social Effects of Highways." *Georgia Highways* (December 1925), vol. 3.

Sprague, Marshall. "First Cars over the Rockies." *Denver Post Empire Magazine*, Aug. 16, 1964.

Stamm, Roy A. "First Autos in Albuquerque." *New Mexico* (February 1953), vol. 31, no. 2.

Taylor, Ralph C. "Car's Advent Brought a Revolution." *Pueblo Chieftain*, Nov. 4, 1973.

Thomas, Charles R. "Road Construction in Dry Regions." *Good Roads* (February 1911), vol. XII, no. 2.

Tilson, George M. "A Brief Historical Account of the Development of Street Pavements with Formula for Calculating the Cost of Maintenance." *Engineering-Contracting* (July 1907), vol. 28, no. 3.

Vincent, H. S. "The Deadwood Good Roads Convention." *Pahasapa Quarterly* (February 1912), vol. 1, no. 2.

Warne, Clinton. "The Acceptance of the Automobile in Nebraska." *Nebraska History*, vol. 37, no. 3.

_____ . "Some effects of the introduction of the automobile on highways and land values in Nebraska." *Nebraska History*, vol. 38, no. 1.

Wharton, Mel. "Road Building with a Ford." *Ford Owner and Dealer* (June 1922), vol. 17, no. 3.

Wood, Ben M. "Good Roads and Highways." *Pahasapa Quarterly* (December 1912), vol. 2, no. 1.

Wood, Henry M. "Hauling Road Materials." *Ford Owner and Dealer* (July 1923), vol. 19.

## Articles, pamphlets, no author given

"Aerial Tramway Across Gila River." *Popular Mechanics* (1915), vol. XXIII.

"Arizona Sweeps Highways to Save Tires for Motorists." *Arizona Highways* (June 1930), vol. VI, no. 6.

"Brick Road Construction." *Good Roads* (November 1913), vol. VI, no. 18.

"Brick Paved Highways in Northern New York." *Good Roads* (March 1, 1913), vol. V, no. 9.

"Building Twenty Miles of Road in a Day." *Topeka Capital*, Jan. 22, 1911.

"The Caterpillar Story." Mimeographed document of 11 pages from the Caterpillar Tractor Co., Inc., Peoria, IL, January 1973.

"The Changing World of Highway Travel." Pamphlet of 34 pages published by R. R. Donnelley, Chicago, to advertise a new style of road maps, 1965.

"Colorado to California in a Model T." *The Runningboard* (March 1974), originally printed in *The Safe Driver*.

"Colorado Works to One Purpose Good Roads Day." *Denver Times*, May 14, 1915.

"Concrete Road Building in Wayne County, Michigan." *Good Roads* (March 1, 1913), vol. V, no. 9.

"Contractors' Equipment." *Good Roads* (May 3, 1913), vol. V, no. 18.

"Convict Labor on Roads." *The Hoosier Motorist*, September 24, 1913.

"Department of Highways History." Commemorative pamphlet on the occasion of the 50th anniversary, South Dakota Department of Highways.

"Desert Road Paved with Asphaltic Concrete." *The Roadrunner* (Nov. 23, 1926), number 61, published by the Asphalt Division of Standard Oil Company of California.

"'Economic' Value of Good Roads." *Scientific American* (June 30, 1900), vol. 49, no. 6.

"First Report of the State Highway Department, 1916-18." Pierre, SD: State of South Dakota, 1918.

"The Ford and the Farmer's Wife." *Ford Times* (1913) vol. 6.

"Ford Power in Road Building and Maintenance." *Ford Owner and Dealer* (May, June, and July 1923) vol. 19.

"Fourth Annual Exhibition of Road Making Machinery, Materials and Appliances." *Good Roads* (Jan. 4, 1913), vol. V, no. 1.

"Good Roads Days." *Good Roads* (Nov. 1, 1913), vol. VI, no. 18.

"The "Good Roads Days' in Missouri." *Good Roads* (Nov. 1, 1913), vol. VI, no. 18.

"Good Roads in Relation to Farm Values." *Scientific American* (March 13, 1897), vol. 43, no. 3.

"Good Roads the Key." *Automobile Topics Daily* (Jan. 16, 1905), vol. 4, no. 1.

"Highway Bridges and Culverts." In J. E. Pennybacker, ed. *Good Roads Year Book of the United States*, American Highway Association, 1913.

"The Huber Story 1863-1948." Pamphlet of 16 pages printed by the Huber Manufacturing Company, Marion, Ohio, 1948.

"The Ideal Road." *Good Roads* (Sept. 6, 1913), vol. VI, No. 10.

"In 1909, Car Made First Trip Through Kentucky Mountains." *Lexington Leader*, June 16, 1940.

"Independents Cut Gas Price." *Sioux Falls Press*, Sept. 20, 1924.

"Indianapolis Industries -- J. D. Adams Graders Are Used All Over the World." *Indianapolis News*, Jan. 8, 1946.

"It Took 63 Days to Make First Auto Crossing of U. S. in 1903." *Denver Post*, May 17, 1953.

"Kansas Trail Markings Blaze Way for Tourists." *Topeka Capital*, Sept. 10, 1919.

"Leaning Wheel Grader Started J. D. Adams." *Indianapolis Star*, Dec. 31, 1947.

"Mark a Trail to Denver: the Golden Belt Road Now Is Ready for Motorists." *Kansas City Star*, June 13, 1912.

"Motor Run a Success." *Sioux Falls Daily Press*, Aug. 22, 1907.

"Narrower Auto Roads." *The Literary Digest* (April 4, 1931), vol. III, no. 13.

"The New York-Chicago Highway." *Automobile Review and Automobile News* (Aug. 15, 1903), vol. 9, no. 4.

"Norbeck Has Auto Record: Senator Was First to Drive Motor from Missouri River to Hills." *Sioux Falls Daily Press*, Sept. 28, 1924.

"'Only Difference Between My First Auto and a Buggy Was the Lack of a Whipsocket on the Dashboard,' Says W. E. Lyman, First Mail Carrier." In Adria Sudlow, ed. *Homestead Years 1908-1968*. Bison, SD: The Bison Courier, 1968.

"Photographic Automobile Map -- Chicago to Rockford, etc." *Photographic Runs Series B*. Chicago: H. Sargent Michaels, Co., 1905.

"The Progress of Good Roads." *Ford Times* (1912), vol 5.

"The Revolution in Road Building. Methods Now in Progress and the Place of John Fitzgerald in Highway History." *Engineering-Contracting* (1908), vol. 30.

"Road Building a Local Affair." *The Hoosier Motorist*, March 24, 1913, originally an editorial in *The Christian Science Monitor*.

"Road Conditions in the West." *Good Roads* (Sept. 2, 1911), vol XIII, no. 9.

"Road Supervisors and Their Failings. As Told by an Eye Witness." *Louisville Automobile Club Toots* (July 1908), vol. 1, no. 5.

"Six Well Traveled Trails Cross Sunflower State from East to West Offering Splendid Routes for Cross-Continental Travel." *Topeka Capital*, May 9, 1915.

"Split Log Drag." Bulletin No. 5, Department of Public Roads, Commonwealth of Kentucky.

"Steel Highway Track." *Automobile Review* (July 23, 1904), vol. 11, no. 4.

"Steel Highways Being Introduced." *Horseless Age* (July 1897), vol. 2, no. 9.

"Sweeping the Highways." *Arizona Highways* (March 1929), vol. V, no. 3.

"To Adopt Plans for Building Road." *Topeka Capital*, Dec. 3, 1911.

"Trail-Blazers Encounter Adventures." *Motor Age* (Sept. 26, 1912), vol. XXII, no. 13.

"Unique Motor Road Opened Across Utah Salt Desert." *New Mexico Highway Journal* (July 1925), vol.

"The Use of Motor Trucks in Road Work." *Good Roads* (May 1913), vol. V, no. 18.

"Used Bands in Road Fight." *Kansas City Times*, Dec. 2, 1911.

"Winds Build Roads in New Mexican Desert." *Colorado Highways Bulletin* (August 1919), vol. II, no. 8.

"Woman Driver Braves the Deep Sands of Arizona." *Ford Times* (1913), vol. 6.

"Wyoming's Highway Development Represents a Steady, Consistent Growth." *Worland Grit*, April 3, 1930.

## Periodicals, multiple relevant articles, without designated author

*American Motorist*

*Auto Era*, publication of the Winton Motor Carriage Co., Cleveland, Ohio.

*Automobile Age*

*The Automobilist*

*Cycle and Automobile Trade Journal*

*Colorado Highway Bulletin* and its successor, *Colorado Highways*

*Facts and Figures of the Automobile Industry*, statistical publication of the National Automobile Chamber of Commerce.

*Ford Owner and Dealer*

*Ford Times*, published by the Ford Motor Co., best and longest lasting of the automobile company house journals.

*Good Roads*

*Good Roads Yearbook*

*Highway Engineer and Contractor*

*Highway Magazine*

*Highways Green Book*, published annually by the American Automobile Association.

*Horseless Age*, the original automobile industry journal.

*Leslie's Weekly*

*McClure's Magazine*

*Motor*

*Motor Age*

*Motor World*

*New Mexico Highway Journal* and its successor, *New Mexico*

*Outing*

*Popular Mechanics*

*Public Roads*

*Roads and Streets* and its succcessor, *Highway and Heavy Construction*

*Scientific American*

*South Dakota Hiway Magazine*

*Southern Good Roads*

*Studebaker Wheel*, publication of the Studebaker Automobile Co., South Bend, Indiana.

*Wyoming State Highway Department Newsletter* and its successor, *Wyoming Roads*

Road maps, with or without guides, from state highway departments, oil companies, and commercial map printers (literally by the hundreds).

# Old Cars Magazines And...

## Guide to Automotive Restoration
- A detailed system-by-system hands-on manual

**ONLY** .................................**$24.95**

## Standard Catalog of 4x4s
- Includes trucks, vans, sports cars built from 1940-1992

**ONLY** .................................**$24.95**

## 100 Years of American Cars
- 500 photo/profiles of America's superstar cars, 1893-1993

**ONLY** .................................**$18.95**

## American Cars, 1946-1975
- More than 1,000 vehicle listings, with pricing

**ONLY** .................................**$27.95**

## American Cars, 1976-1986
- Pinpoints tomorrw's collector cars today, with pricing

**ONLY** .................................**$19.95**

## Standard Catalog of Ford
- All data, codes, explanations, specifications and pricing

**ONLY** .................................**$19.95**

## Standard Catalog of Chevrolet
- Fascinating stories and historical profiles, with pricing

**ONLY** .................................**$19.95**

## Standard Catalog of Chrysler
- 1990 values through 1983 models, with pricing

**ONLY** .................................**$19.95**

## Standard Catalog of Buick
- Chassis specs, body types, shipping weights and pricing

**ONLY** .................................**$18.95**

## Standard Catalog of Cadillac
- All the photos, profiles, techs & specs, with pricing

**ONLY** .................................**$18.95**

## American Light-Duty Trucks
- More than 500 truck listings from 1896-1986, 2nd Edition

**ONLY** .................................**$29.95**

## Police Cars: A Photographic History
- Profiles from the Keystone Cop cars to Corvette Cop cars

**ONLY** .................................**$14.95**

## Old Cars Weekly
- Your collector car news & marketplace resource

**1 Year (52 issues)** .................**$29.95**

## Old Cars Price Guide
- Your bi-monthly collector car price guide authority

**1 Year (6 issues)** ...................**$16.95**

# Krause Publications
**700 E. State St., Iola, WI 54990-0001**

*Add $2.50 shipping for each book ordered!*

**MasterCard/VISA Cardholders**
**Order Toll-Free By Calling...**
# 800-258-0929
Dept. ACY, Mon.-Fri., 6:30 am - 8 pm, Sat. 8 am - 2 pm, CST